# CINCINNATI DOE:

# A MOTHER'S 30-DAY JOURNEY IN ICU

By Donna M. Haynes

# DISCLAIMER

This memoir is a truthful recollection of actual events in the author's life. Some of the events, places and conversations have been recreated and/or supplemented from memory. The chronology of some events has been compressed. When necessary, the names and identifying details of some individuals have been changed to maintain anonymity and respect their privacy.

This book is inspired by and dedicated to the strongest person that I know.
My son, Cameron.
#CamStrong

"Maybe you went through it and survived it
just so you could help someone else make it through."
-Unknown

# TABLE OF CONTENTS

# ACKNOWLEDGEMENTS

I will be forever indebted to the medical staff and health practitioners that saved my son's life at the Prince George's Hospital Trauma Center and the National Rehabilitation Hospital. My gratitude is extended to the team of surgeons, doctors, nurses, technicians, therapists, chaplains, security guards, administrators—to all who played a role in his journey to recovery. Whether you laid a hand on this patient or simply offered a kind word in passing…you mattered, and we will never forget you. Please accept my sincere apologies if my mixed emotions during this unsettling experience ever displayed anything different.

Until my dying day, I will never be able to find the words to properly describe the appreciation I have for my parents Donald and Diana Haynes. From DAY ONE, the pair has been my biggest cheerleading team, and they have set an exemplary standard for me as a parent, a friend, a professional, and an overall good human being. As grandparents, they've never missed a single game, ceremony, performance, or celebratory occasion. Thank you for always encouraging my dreams and for walking with me through the nightmares.

A very special thanks to the friends, co-workers, and family who supported my son and me through the most difficult time of our lives. Because of you, I could bear to stomach another day. Faces that I hadn't seen in years showed up to extend residual love that stemmed from timeless sowed seeds. You all proved that when we are good to others, our blessings are returned tenfold.

My class is better than yours! The Largo High School Class of 1989 rallied around me like a pillar of steel, providing the necessary strength in numbers while I was in my darkest hour. Special thanks to Belinda for spearheading the #CamStrong campaign, to Travis and Butler Signs for expediting the envisioned paraphernalia, to Yolanda for being a financial sponsor, and to my classmates for the donations, prayers, and endless love.

To my college sisters, my tribe, the loves of my life, my Pearl Team, the blood sisters that I never had...I check yet another box to indicate how we've collectively supported one another. Through thirty years of bad hairstyles, bad boyfriends, and just plain bad decisions, you each have always helped me to SEE IT THROUGH...literally. From the Alpha to the Omega, and back to the Omega again, you each have my HEARTfelt thanks...for everything.

My Best Friends,
*Gwen:* From the sandbox to the bookshelves, thank you for being a leader and for reminding me that it's important to speak my truth. You continue to set an impeccable standard for women of strength everywhere.

*Derwinn:* Thank you for always being the first to show up...no matter what. You, my friend, are the big brother that every girl prays for.

*Kisha:* Whether it be for emergency, action, or no-judgement advice...you are my Go-To Girl. Thank you for always seeing the good in me, even when I struggle to see it within myself. You love me on the days that I'm unlovable and push me to be great in a way that only a Boo-Thang can.

*Tom:* Timing is everything. God saw fit to bring you into my life at a moment that He knew I would need an intimate partner most. I cannot imagine how I could have survived this experience without you. Thanks for sticking it out with us on this wild ride!

Stacie, I love and miss you. But I know that I've had my own personal Guardian Angel since the day you departed this earth. I'd give anything to talk to you these days. However, I'm thankful for the peace that I feel just knowing that you are always watching and helping to guide my steps along the way. I pray that I am making you proud, Sis.

To my first born, David…though I know your hurt runs as deep as mine some days, I thank you for growing up and standing on your own two feet during a time that I needed you to the most. You give me so much hope for the next generation, and I could not be prouder of who you've become as son, a brother, a leader, and a MAN! Keep reaching for the stars, Son.

To my community of TBI (Traumatic Brain Injury) survivors who have endured comparable experiences, and their caregivers (especially mothers) who share similar stories and feelings—although it seems at times you are in an isolated place of existence which causes you to feel so alone, you are not alone.

And last, but certainly not least, thank you Lord for not only sparing my son, but for giving me the opportunity to be his mother. You gave me the support, strength, and resources that were necessary in providing the best care for him. I questioned my faith a time or two during this walk. But through you, it has since been reinforced, and I now know firsthand that MIRACLES ARE REAL. YOU are a Way Maker, and I will never doubt your power again.

# PROLOGUE

On August 4, 2018, I received the call that every mother on the planet dreads. My son had been critically injured. And at that very moment, my life would no more be what it was prior to the ring of my cell phone that day. My priorities, my areas of knowledge and expertise, my thought patterns...all became different. Even the way I view LIFE has changed drastically. Instead of sweating the small stuff, I've learned to celebrate small successes because they turn into blessings that later become miracles.

I'm a firm believer that everything happens for a reason, whether or not we can understand or accept it at the time. Our stories are already written and extraordinarily planned out to the tee, long before our existence even occurs. And as difficult as this journey has been, I have been enlightened along the way by how amazingly everything continues to fall into place.

Though our story is nothing short of unforgettable, I thank God I had the wherewithal to journalize this experience each day—recording almost every step in its truest form. The described life events are told in a mother's first-person narrative. Speaking directly to my son, the outlined vantage point relays detail around his display of resilience, shedding light on why he is viewed as a warrior of inspiration.

Writing this manuscript has allowed me to fully grieve in the way that I needed but couldn't while weathering the storm. The recent global COVID-19 pandemic and related quarantine forced me to not only be still in my thoughts, but it also afforded me the opportunity to capture them and therapeutically express some misplaced, suppressed emotions.

Through my son's tragedy, I've recognized my purpose.

Sure, it's easy to focus on the obvious issues that afflict our communities, our country, and our world. To speak up and take a stance on the daily trends that monopolize our newsfeeds and saturate the media outlets for a spell is simple. But to represent an unpopular pain and struggle, even when your voice seems small and unheard, is an unexplainably difficult calling that I vow to never stop answering. As long as I have breath in my body, I will be a dedicated advocate for survivors of traumatic brain injury, victims of senseless gun violence, and the challenges that are relative to each of them.

As a member of many support groups, hearing other stories of triumph, love, patience, fear, resilience, and courage truly gave me the hope that I needed in some very hopeless moments. Therefore, it is important that I share this experience with others because the stories that others have previously shared helped me to survive my own trauma.

This powerful recollection is sure to give way to discussion around many related topics such as brain injury, caregiving, gun violence, and the shared fears of motherhood. And though my son vaguely remembers any of it, I pray that the written outline of his story will also serve as part of his healing process and give him a greater understanding of our journey together during a time of crisis.

The obvious and more visible parts of my son's recovery generally leave people speechless, reminding them to never give up, regardless of how grim a circumstance. However, after learning about some of the more intimate details, readers will know this theory to be even more true. An unsure mother, a frustrated caregiver, or simply an average Joe who is struggling from a life-altering setback can benefit from the will to live that is described in this story. Miracles are real, and there is hope in healing.

# DAY 1

## A MOTHER'S WORST NIGHTMARE

I am in no way, shape, or form a morning person. But dragging myself out of bed at 5:45 a.m. was nothing compared to the new, scary journey that Jill had ahead of her. Sitting with her through her first round of chemotherapy was the least I could do. I could only imagine how nervous she was to start the road of battling Stage III breast cancer, but I planned to help see her through it every step of the way. The 60-minute drive to the Woodburn Infusion Center in the wee hours of the morning was just the first step.

I reached for my cell phone to turn off the annoying ringtone that I'd selected as an alarm. *NOTE TO SELF: Change that blowhorn ringtone to something less annoying*, I thought, as I lay my head back on my pillow. I closed my eyes and whispered, "Thank you for waking me up, Lord." With my eyes still closed, I smiled inside, thinking about last night's date with my new guy. He'd taken me to a random seafood restaurant in Virginia, and we'd tried new foods together. He had never eaten fried alligator before, and I was impressed with his attempt to impress me by trying it. For our next date, we agreed that I would choose the restaurant.

*NOTE TO SELF: Google restaurants with views by the water.*

With the cell phone still in my hand, I exhaled and tapped the home security app to scan the recent activity on the alarm system. I did this every morning to see if you'd made it in by your 2 a.m. curfew. There had been no activity since 11:00 p.m. last night when I got home from my date. *I know this boy didn't stay out all night.*

I swiped over to my phone calls...and there were no missed calls from you in the log. I swiped to my text messages—again, nothing from you. "I'm gonna wring his neck!" I angrily thought out loud.

Of my two children, you've always been the one to push the envelope every chance you had. You kept me on my mental toes, and I had to stay two steps ahead of you at all times. After a while, you were no longer surprised when I popped up at locations you thought were confidential. I was once your age, Son, and girls are smarter. You were a rising sophomore at the local community college, scheduled to take more classes in the fall, while continuing to work your part-time job. At age 19, you enjoyed teenage life whenever you could, although you definitely liked to taste the adult life every now and then. Even still, you lived under my roof, which meant you had to respect and abide by my rules.

Further annoyed, I flung the covers to the side of the bed and sprung to my feet in a single bound like a superhero who just received a call of trouble, and it was her job to save the day. All mothers of teenagers are familiar with this leading role and infamous move. I marched down the dark, narrow hallway, passing your bathroom that was lit by a decorative nightlight.

Once I arrived at your bedroom door, your perfectly made bed confirmed that you had not been home. Shaking my head and rolling my eyes, I immediately grabbed my cell phone again to call you several times—no answer.

"Welp," I sighed. I decided to call your father. It was 5:55 a.m. on a Saturday morning, so I knew I'd be disturbing him from something.

"Hey. Sorry to bother you. Cameron didn't come home last night. Have you heard from him?" I asked, hoping that he had.

It turned out that I wasn't disturbing him at all. He had recently and unexpectedly relocated to Philadelphia on a work assignment, but oddly enough, he was in town and on his way to a couple of leisure rounds of golf at a nearby course.

"No, I haven't talked to him since yesterday afternoon. But I will try calling him myself, and I'll call David, too, to find out if he has heard from him."

I stood in the middle of my bathroom floor and stared in the mirror for a couple of minutes, a little torn on what to do next. *Do I still meet Jill at the hospital? Or do I sit still and wait to hear from you?* I texted you to ask that you check in just to let me know that you were okay. As I showered, my mind scrambled a million miles per minute in an organized mess:

*Who should I call?*
*Where could Cameron be?*
*Lord, I hope he wasn't in a car accident and in a ditch on the side of the road somewhere.*

I stopped lathering and began praying. I leaned against the cold tile wall, letting the hot water from the shower spray my back.

Shortly afterward, I threw on my favorite pair of black leggings, a crop top T-shirt that hit right at the waistline, and a long-sleeved jean shirt to cover my arms, just in case it was chilly in the medical center. While I assembled a care package for Jill that included Cheez-Its, mixed nuts, and a pink breast cancer metal bottle filled with cold water, I continued to call your cell phone. Your father and brother David both called to say that neither had heard from you. No one was able to reach you.

As I drove slowly up a deserted Branch Avenue at 7:00 a.m. en route to my friend, I scanned the road, hoping not to see a mangled black sedan on the side of the highway. I remembered that you were scheduled to be at work early that morning, so I called your job to ask if you were there. Your supervisor, Grant, said he had not heard from you. The little hope that I'd been holding on to went out the window at that point. You loved that job. And if nowhere else, that's the one place you would happily report to on time. When you got off work the night before, you'd called to tell me about a new skill you'd learned and just how much you were enjoying the experience. I asked Grant to have you contact me once you arrived at work, and then worry and fear immediately set in as I disconnected the call.

I began calling the local hospitals to inquire about a "Cameron Daniels." I was somewhat relieved as each receptionist did not find your name on their registry. But a numb feeling began to take over. My foot suddenly turned into a brick on the gas pedal, and I seemed to make it to the medical center in no time.

I painted on my usual smile of hope and support when I entered the waiting room to meet Jill and her mom. We shared hugs, laughs, and appropriate banter for the reason we were there. After Jill was called back to the treatment room where she'd be settling in for her procedure, I had a chance to sit and talk with Ms. Gloria for a while. I had absolutely no intentions of sharing with her or Jill what was currently happening with me. It was Jill's day. And I was there to support her.

Ms. Gloria, however, shared her concerns with me about Jill and her health, how she may have gotten sick, and how they were both dealing with it all. I always enjoy talking with Jill's mother. She's so full of wisdom and hope. She didn't even know how she was giving me inspiration in that very moment to cope with my own fears that were looming in my spirit. I was a wreck on the inside, but on the outside, I maintained my composure. Despite my frantic worry, when the nurse called us into the treatment room to be with Jill, I walked in with Ms. Gloria as if nothing was wrong.

Jill's hair was flowing, and her lipstick was popping, drawing less attention to all the tubes, monitors, and machines she was hooked up to. She enjoyed her snacks and reminisced on funny memories, and her head bobbed every now and then as she napped. I held her hand for some time, but was glad that she had fallen off to sleep so that I could pull out my laptop. I needed to open the "Find My iPhone" application to try searching your location online. Unfortunately, I couldn't figure out how to use the service, so that was a completely busted effort.

I looked at the clock on the wall and realized the entire morning had passed. At 11:00 a.m., there was still no word from you. I continued to text with David, who had begun to contact your friends. I walked in and out of the treatment room so that I could take calls from your father. He'd pulled your cell phone records, so we decided to split the list of numbers and call them. Your friends couldn't reach you, your supervisor still hadn't heard from you, and the people on your phone log were shady and unhelpful.

*Keep it together, Donna,* I thought, as I returned to the treatment room with Jill and continued texting various people. By then, though I hadn't said a word, Jill and her mom knew something was wrong.

I helplessly looked at the clock again; it was 1:00 p.m. My cell phone vibrated with an incoming call from your father, and I quickly ran out of the treatment room to answer.

"The police just left my house. Cameron has been shot. He's alive and at P.G. Hospital."

My screams filled the hallway of the medical center, but my tear ducts had not quite caught up with the emotion that had taken over.

"I'M ON MY WAY!" I shouted. And I was.

Your father didn't know much more than what he had told me, but I knew I needed to get to P.G. Hospital immediately. Still trying to maintain what little composure I could muster, I walked back into the treatment room where Jill and Ms. Gloria sat quietly. As I began frantically packing my things, I managed to utter, "Jill...I'm sorry, but I have to go. I haven't said anything, but Cameron has been missing all morning. We just found out that he's been shot, so I have to get to the hospital." I honestly don't know what the ladies' responses were because in that moment, they both sounded like Charlie Brown's schoolteacher. *Womp Womp Womp Womp Womp Womp.*

Needless to say, I flew out of the parking lot, skidding on two wheels like a bat out of hell. Speeding from one hospital to another, I clutched my steering wheel as firmly as I could. I screamed, cried, and hollered out to you at the top of my lungs:

"CAMERON! PLEASE BE OKAY! MOMMY IS COMING, SON! I'M COMING FOR YOU! LORD, PLEASE COVER MY CHILD! WHATEVER THE SITUATION, FATHER GOD, HAVE HIM KNOW THAT HE CAN LEAN ON YOU RIGHT NOW! LET HIM KNOW THAT I'M COMING, DEAR LORD!"

I was able gather myself enough to make three phone calls:

*My Parents:* Nana answered the phone in her usual pleasant Saturday afternoon voice, "Hi, Donna!" It tore me apart to ask her to sit down so that I could immediately change her mood with this news. But like the rock that I'd always known Diana to be, I heard her say, "Donald, Cameron has been shot. We have to get to the hospital." Before she hung up, she calmly told me that she was putting on her shoes and that she and Granddaddy were heading out.

*Last Night's Date:* Tom was one of the first people I texted when I realized you hadn't come home, and he had been checking in every hour on the hour. So, when he answered my call, he sounded like he was expecting it. "Good news?" Saying the words out of my mouth hurt even more the second time. After telling him what I knew and where I was going, he told me that he was on the way.

*My Best Friend:* Kisha was part of a group chat with our college girlfriends, The Pearls. A few hours prior, I'd asked them for prayer because you were missing. I knew that in calling Kisha with this news, she'd know how to contact my immediate circle of friends, and the word would then spread to everyone else who needed to know. She immediately left home to meet me at the hospital, too.

My originating location in Virginia was probably farther away from anyone else's; yet, I arrived at Prince George's Hospital Center before all of them! I ran into the Emergency Room entrance and inquired about you with the receptionist. When she told me that they didn't have anyone by the name of *Cameron Daniels*, my venom immediately began to rise, filling my mouth and waiting on the back of my teeth. In the nick of time, your father walked in, saving the receptionist from my wrath. Always thinking quickly on his feet, he suggested maybe you could be listed as a "John Doe." I impatiently watched the receptionist slowly browse the files without any sense of care or urgency…and *VOILÀ*, three John Does had been brought into ICU throughout the night. As your grandparents walked in with long, concerned faces, the hospital administrator Caren asked me for a photo of you so that she could verify your identification. Upon confirmation, we were all escorted to the Trauma Center of the hospital. You had been admitted as "Cincinnati Doe."

Your grandparents were directed to the waiting room, and your father and I were escorted back to your room in ICU—Bed #5. One of the nurses stopped us just outside of your room to clearly explain why you were in critical care: You'd been shot in the head. *In. The. Head.*

*OH MY GOD!*

I think all the blood left my brain at that very moment, and I wasn't quite sure that I could actually walk into your room.

The nurse said you'd be unable to talk to us, and you were hooked up to several tubes and machines. Your father hugged me and asked me if I could handle it. I'd never felt weaker, but I knew that you needed my strength…so I agreed to continue to Bed #5. Several doctors and nurses were gathered around the room, waiting for us to come in so they could explain your status. We were in disbelief at what we saw.

You'd just gotten a fresh haircut the day before. But now, one side of your head was completely shaved, partially covered with a bandage that needed to be changed because it accumulated a lot of blood. Several tubes protruded from your head, crisscrossing in every direction and connecting to a number of machines and plastic blood-filled bulbs. Your face was slightly swollen, and it was covered in several deep, red nicks and cuts. Though your eyes were completely closed, I could tell they were both puffy. Your mouth was propped wide open with a tube that looked as if it had been shoved down your throat, and a T-like strap was laid horizontally on top of it to hold the heavy plastic in place. Uncontrollable saliva fell from your full lips, which were covered in a Vaseline-like substance, and your exposed tongue hung with no purpose. A neck brace elevated your chin and made you look as stiff as a corpse. I could see the tubes of the ventilator shake every time it rhythmically pumped air into your body. Your feet and legs were covered, but I could clearly see that your arms lay lifeless, along with every other exposed part of your body. No matter how hard I've tried since, I will never forget that image.

The doctor started explaining your condition, but the more she talked, the more she sounded like Charlie Brown's teacher. *When did she get here?* I felt sick. *Was this real? Was I dreaming?* The room became unsteady, and I fainted. Thank goodness your father remained present and was able to receive all the information that the doctor provided and also ask questions.

As for me? The nurses put my limp body in a wheelchair, covered me in cold compresses and blankets, and gave me iced water. I was having an out-of-body experience and could barely look at you through my squinted eyes that were now clouded with tears and sweat. I wanted desperately to wake up from this unbearable night terror that was occurring in the middle of a sunny Saturday afternoon.

Someone had tried to rob you and shot you in the back of the head. You'd apparently driven away after being shot, hit several cars on the street in a residential neighborhood in Clinton, Maryland, and crashed into someone's yard. The ruckus startled several neighbors, who immediately called the police. Paramedics transported you to the hospital and reported that you were actually talking when you arrived. Dr. Maria Nesby immediately began emergency surgery as you started to lose consciousness.

The bullet entered the right side of your cerebellum but fortunately did not penetrate too deeply. Part of your skull was removed to allow the necessary spacing for your brain to swell after surgery. The medical team said that you were responsive post-surgery. Fragments of the bullet were left in your head because they were pretty deep, and the surgeon did not want to potentially cause any further damage. You were heavily sedated by the time we saw you, and we were told that the next 72 hours were crucial in determining your survival.

I managed to clearly hear a voice asking about your "health insurance coverage," and that's when I snapped out of my fog. I couldn't believe the lack of compassion, but I guess it was hospital protocol.

I spoke up with relief and a sense of pride and offered to

provide the requested information. "Yes, he has insurance!" A clipboard was shoved in my face while I still sat in the wheelchair that had caught my fall just 15 minutes prior. I whipped out my insurance card so the staff administration could record the needed account numbers; then suddenly, I knew that you would get the best care possible.

Your father and I were directed to the ICU waiting room, and waiting for us were Granddaddy, Nana, Derwinn, Kisha, and last night's date, Tom Ford (as you called him). We stood and gave them a collective update on you, repeating everything the doctors had told us and answering all of their questions the best we could. Because I'd blacked out and didn't get all of the details, your father did most of the talking. The much-needed hugs from our loved ones outshined the looks of despair and feelings of concern.

As we sat and waited in disbelief throughout the day, a number of people trickled in to show their support…each face longer than the next: your brother, David, Tia, Reggie, Ronald, Lennox and Jeffrey, Coach Phil, Aunt Ann, Jasmine, Ms. Stacye and Jamal, Lafayette, Curt, Gwen, Pastor Ron, Belinda, and Mike.

I don't see or talk to your Uncle Kevin for years at a time, so I was surprised to also see him in the waiting room. My brother and I have had an estranged relationship because of our differences in parenting, religion, and just about everything two people can disagree on. As a teenager, I admired my one and only sibling and secretly had the utmost respect for him. He was funny, charismatic, handsome, and had all the answers, or so I thought. But as time progressed and life happened, our journeys unfortunately took us down different paths that didn't allow me to see him in the same light. However, when he stood in the ICU lobby of the hospital and cried over what had happened to you, every onlooker who knew our history couldn't maintain a dry eye as we embraced and temporarily put our differences aside. I was glad he came.

Lennox offered a powerful prayer over our family before he left mid-day. Later, Pastor Ron ended the evening with a group prayer, and we all joined hands, stretching the entire circumference of the waiting room.

*How can I leave you here, Son?*

A mother should never have to experience this. I was afraid to look at you, afraid to touch you, and afraid to even talk to you. I was still hoping that I was in a horrific dream that would not be real once I woke up.

David kept my car, and Tom drove me home so that I could pack some clothes and stay at his house for a while, since it's only a 10-minute drive from the hospital, and my house is an hour away. During the drive, I was silent. I had an opportunity to finally scroll through the dozens of unanswered text messages and compose a copy-and-paste generic response to provide the most appropriate information at the time. This would become part of my routine most nights, just to keep people whom I knew anxiously awaited an updated report.

Walking into my dark house, I turned on the light in the foyer that you'd always turn off when you came home each night.

*NOTE TO SELF: Keep this light on until Cameron comes home again.*

The house was eerily quiet, but I slowly walked up all 29

stairs from the basement, making a beeline to my bedroom on the top level. I shoved my toiletries, undergarments, and an array of leggings, sweatpants, and T-shirts in a random bag, then I walked down that narrow hallway again, headed to your room. Somehow, I was again hoping to find you there, sleeping peacefully. I turned on the light, and just sat still on your bed for a couple of minutes before grabbing some items from your nightstand and dresser drawers:

- one of your favorite stretchy bracelets, that I quickly snapped around my left hand and slid up my wrist;
- one of your high school senior pictures—an 8x10 of the traditional pose, wearing your black cap & gown;
- a 5x7 picture from the same senior package—you are dressed in black slacks and a black button-down shirt, straddling a chair, holding your baseball bat, and wearing black-rimmed personality glasses.

As a senior in high school just the year before, you were the captain of the baseball team. Popular, funny, and full of personality. I wanted to put these pictures in your hospital room so that the doctors, nurses, and technicians could all see what you looked like, and who you really were. You were NOT just another unidentified black boy with a traumatic gunshot wound who did not have a life, one whom no one cared about.

You were NOT "Cincinnati Doe." You ARE someone's son, brother, grandson, cousin, nephew, teammate, and friend. And, you are loved.

# DAY 2

## THE NIGHTMARE BECOMES A NEW REALITY

Before I could even open my eyes the next morning, I prayed that the entire day before had been just a bad dream. But as I lay frozen, I remembered the reason I'd spent the night at Tom's house and not my own: *Cameron. My baby. Somebody shot my baby!* Tears rolled down my face and saturated the pillow as I replayed moments from the day in my mind. It all seemed like a blur...yet, I remembered everything so vividly. I thought about the number of doctors, nurses, and administrators I'd encountered—the way you were hooked up to all the machines and tubes. I recalled all the people who visited the hospital to support our family throughout the day. *Have I notified everyone?* I reached for my l cell phone to compose an email to my immediate work family through foggy, blood-shot eyes. This group of people was my team in every sense of the word, and I'd realized they didn't know what had happened. No one knew to reach out to any of them. After I hit "Send" on a frank, straightforward email, I pulled the covers over my head and prayed again, while crying uncontrollably. This was real.

During the quick drive to the hospital, I scarfed down as much as I could of the breakfast sandwich and coffee that Tom had prepared for me. I hopped out of the passenger seat with a deep sigh and headed into the front doors of the hospital to get a visitor's badge at the security desk.

You were finally listed in the hospital's registry under your real name, and I was noted as "The Mother." It was a long walk from the entrance of the hospital to the trauma center area, but I broke up the journey with a stop at the gift shop. As I paid for the small metal cross that I planned to put in your room, I heard a deep, familiar voice ask, "How are you doing?" It was Carlos! My team member, co-worker, little brother of a friend had beaten me to the hospital after reading my early morning email.

Carlos and I had worked together for about 15 years in different areas of the union. I'd watched him grow up from a 19-year-old, snotty-nosed, cornrow and jersey-wearing kid who thought he knew it all, to a mature husband and father of 3, whom colleagues requested to partner with because of his knowledge, professionalism, and work ethic. He was like the "cool uncle" to you and David, and he had watched you both grow up from toddlers to young men. Though it was good to see 'Los, I really didn't know what to say to him. My email was self-explanatory, and the look on his face told me that I didn't need to say a word. He was there to be supportive and offer me a hug.

Because it was so early, I took Carlos with me to your room so that he could see you. I'd warned him of the grim state you were in so that he'd know what to expect before entering ICU. After I told Caren that Carlos was your uncle, the secured doors buzzed and swung open. We slowly approached Bed #5.

Standing over you for just a couple of seconds, all your uncle could do was shake his head in disgust. "Ridiculous," he said, and walked out of the room. He asked me the million-dollar question that everyone wanted answered: "WHAT HAPPENED?"

But at that time, I didn't have any relative information

for my friend who had visibly become angry from the mere idea that someone would do this to you. And as anxious as I was to get to the bottom of what landed you there, my main focus was your survival during those critical hours.

Later that morning, your father and I put the pictures and inspirational quotes around your room that we each had brought from our homes. We spoke with Chara, your day nurse, as well as with the attending physician on duty. They explained that your Intracranial Pressure (ICP) was at 30, which was extremely high, considering 7 - 15 is the normal ranging measurement. This pressure is determined by existing fluid inside the skull and on the brain tissue. You were given a different medication to try to decrease the duress in your head, as well as your spiking blood pressure. I prayed that it would work.

Eventually, we spoke with Dr. Maria Nesby, the surgeon who had operated on you when you were admitted, and she gave us a good report. Though you weren't completely out of the woods, she was confident you were going to make it. She said that when you'd been taken off sedation, you were intermittently responding to commands, moving your limbs, and opening your eyes. The doctor explained that the part of your brain that was injured was the least dominant. Though you still could not move your left arm, the surgeon did not think it was a result of paralysis because you could move your left leg. This was positive news. I noticed Dr. Nesby gazing at the photos that were displayed in your room. "Your son's youth and athleticism will definitely play a major role in his recovery. He's a very strong young man," she said. *Thank you, Lord,* I silently prayed.

By mid-afternoon, the medical staff was finally able to get your pressure down, and they wanted you to rest.

Though you were heavily sedated and unable to communicate, you could still sense the traffic of visitors in and out of your room. Your father and I decided to gather all of the visitors who filled the waiting room to make a few announcements.

We shared the surgeon's positive report, along with our decision to restrict visitation to your bedside for the remainder of the day, allowing you to maintain a calm and quiet environment. Outside of David, your father, your grandparents, and me, no one else could see you. I heard claps and shouts of celebration and praise of the promising news, which prompted Granddaddy to lead a prayer that sounded throughout the entire waiting room. Even people who were visiting other patients joined our circle of prayer. No one was overwhelmingly disappointed that they were unable to see you. People just wanted to be close by to offer their love and support. There were smiles, hugs, and sighs of a little relief all over the room from your visiting friends and family: Carlos, Stevie, Lynn, Wade & Dana, Cliff, Stephanie, Roz, Robin, Deon, Coach Phil & Peggy, Aunt Pat and the Usher Board, , Nichelle and Marcus, Kim, Makeba, Kisha and Adrian, Aunt Ann, Carmen, Belinda, Brian S. and his niece, Brian E., Rod, Mike L., Buff, Faison, Justice, Domo and Latonia, Josh, Zaylah, Jessica, Ernest, and Andrea.

Most everyone parted ways after hearing the positive news. Many returned to their homes or continued enjoying their usual Sunday evenings. But those of us who chose to hang around just needed to take a break from the waiting room. A handful of my girlfriends joined me in the small café located on the first floor of the hospital. Since Makeba and Kim had traveled all the way from Baltimore, they maximized their trip by staying behind to encourage me to eat something.

Though I don't see your father's best friend's wife too often since the divorce, Ms. Peggy was also by my side at that moment, as she's always been when it came to supporting our family. We all enjoyed some good laughs, smiles, and several orders of french fries while sitting at the small, uneven metal table that wobbled every time each one of us reached for a fry. I was emotionally exhausted but happy to be surrounded with so much "Girl Power."

I FaceTimed with my cousin, LeAnn, who was in Punta Cana for her honeymoon, and also with a third Baltimorean girlfriend, Leah, who was on vacation in Bermuda. I gave them both the encouraging news, and they each assured me that they would visit as soon as they returned to the States.

Before getting back on the road, Makeba and Kim walked with Peggy and me back to the ICU waiting room to grab their things and say their final goodbyes for the evening. Your father was sitting in one of the chairs with his back facing the door, and the girls walked down the back aisle to tell him goodbye. I noticed a woman sitting next to him, and assumed it was one of his many co-workers who had come by the hospital for support.

"Donna, I want you to meet someone," your father said with a weird tone in his voice. Every woman knows the tone. "Donna, this is Alisa. Alisa, this is Donna."

My initial response was automatic; it was the same generic response that I gave everyone he'd introduced to me over the last 24 hours. But then my instinct and memory bank kicked in within 1.5 seconds. I'd heard her name from you and David when you had accidentally mentioned her existence in random conversation.

"Alisa? Ohhhhh…you're the girlfriend?" I asked, with a wide smile while bending down to be eye-level with her. She did not have enough respect to even stand up to greet the grieving mother, as everyone else had done.

Clueless, Alisa perked up with a proud smile and replied, "YES!"

My painted-on smile immediately turned to disgust, and I said to her with a stern protective mother's tone, "How dare you be here!"

I quickly cut my eyes at your father and sharply said to him, "And how dare YOU bring her here!"

My ex-husband and I had only been officially divorced for about six months, according to signed and stamped court documents and legal paperwork. However, prior to that, we had been officially separated for almost a year. During the four years leading up to our separation, our marriage had been pretty rocky. I was finally fed up from the years of infidelity and learning about various women that he'd entertained. Checking phone logs and cursing out random heifers had become exhausting, and I was convinced that I deserved better. Though Alisa appeared to be his last adulterous conquest, she was definitely one of many throughout our 22-year union.

Women, especially wives, can be better investigators than any FBI agent with a top-secret clearance and a 30-year retirement package. I had done my research and knew all about Miss Alisa: where she lived, where she worked, about her children, about her divorce, and how long my then-husband had been creeping with her.

Ironically, her short blonde "natural" afro, red reading glasses, and 5-foot-nothing stature was familiar…go figure.

As Alisa quickly scrambled to gather her things, she nervously responded, "I'll leave."

"Yes, you do that."

But in Alisa's defense, her boyfriend extended his arm across her body as if to protect her from what he knew could possibly be next. He said, "No. You don't have to go anywhere."

It was obvious that your father had not fully disclosed to his mistress neither the temperament of his ex-wife nor the circumstances. He'd somehow convinced her that it was okay to be at the hospital with a mother who was distressed over potentially losing her child, who just also happened to be the same woman whose husband she'd cheated with. And she was either that in love…or that stupid…to fall for it. Or both.

"Yes, you do need to leave. Now!" I demanded, then turned to your father and pointed. "Our son is in there fighting for his life right now, and you bring *this* in here!? Really, Gary?"

As I began to leave the waiting room to compose my emotions, my ex-husband stood and screamed behind my head to try to justify his poor decision. I didn't have to say anything further though because the mother, wife, and Baltimore came out of Makeba as she planted herself in front of him to speak in my defense.

"Uh…no, Gary. You're not going to do that. You're not going to talk to her like that. You're dead wrong."

The aisle of uncomfortable chairs became quite noisy, as

Alisa bumped into all of them to scurry out of the waiting room, her boyfriend following close behind.

I sat down to gather myself, and my girlfriends rallied around me in amazement, including Ms. Peggy. She was probably more of a friend to your father than to me. However, she is a woman and wife first, and she understood just how disrespectful that scene was.

*Unbelievable. This was definitely not the time to show off his not-so-new love. What was he thinking?,* I wondered as I breathed deeply.

Well, Gary shortly returned to the waiting room to grab his backpack that he'd mistakenly left behind…and he used that as the opportunity to tell me exactly what he was thinking. Making a beeline over to where I was sitting, my ex-husband stood over me and exclaimed, "Thanks a lot, Donna!"

"Thanks? For what?" I asked.

"Thanks for being an ass!"

"Are you serious? Why would you bring your mistress in here and flaunt her in my face, Gary?! How disrespectful!"

"I didn't say anything when you brought your lil' boyfriend in here yesterday!" he countered.

*WHOOMP, there it is!* He was jealous! Really? The guy I was newly dating had rushed to the hospital after my son was shot, and my cheating ex-husband of over 20 years was jealous. Just. Wow.

"Gary, I've been dating that man for less than three

months. You've been screwing that bitch for over three years—while we were married! There's a huge difference."

At that moment, I tuned him completely out. I honestly don't remember anything he said after that, as Charlie Brown's teacher always seemed to show up at the most inopportune times. However, I clearly heard Ms. Peggy speak up and tell your father that he was wrong and that he needed to leave. He took her advice, put his tail between his legs, and with what little dignity he had left, walked out of the waiting room. It wouldn't be until later that I realized he'd also left the hospital for the evening to be consoled by his mistress, leaving his son fighting for his life in the ICU. David and I spent the next three hours at your bedside so that you wouldn't be alone.

Later as I prepared to leave, your pressure levels had elevated, and the right side of your face had significantly swollen. I was worried, and I didn't want to leave you. Inga, your night nurse, walked me through the process of what she'd do to regulate your numbers, and assured me that you would be fine. This was normal. She promised to call during the night to give me an update, regardless of the news. My heart told me that you were in good hands. I prayed over you and rubbed the anointing oil that Pastor Ron had given to me on your head, hands, and feet, your bed, and in the doorway of your room. David scribbled a very appropriate poem on the back of an envelope and pinned it on the foot of your bed. He'd learned the passage some time ago and recited it often during many of his own uncertain, difficult times.

***BE STRONG. For we are not here to play, dream, or drift. We have hard work to do and many loads to lift. We shall not struggle, for it is God's gift... to be strong.***

David, my firstborn, has dealt with his own set of turmoil throughout his young adult life. He'd graduated just three years ago from a prestigious, diverse Catholic High school with academic honors, a favorable athletic experience, and a new-found love for the performing arts. However, during his first week of college at an HBCU in Delaware, he was assaulted and robbed at gunpoint on campus. Mentally and emotionally, he was bruised pretty badly for a while, but certainly not broken. Over time, he had since re-routed his rage and disappointment and was all set to begin his senior year at a different institution in the fall. My son had been able to surround himself with encouraging people who pushed him to be better. He learned to passionately express himself in a way that is nurturing, sincere, and infectious. You needed your big brother more than ever, and that simple, but powerful poem was just the beginning.

As promised, Nurse Inga called me in the middle of the night to let me know that your pressure had stabilized, and you were resting well. *You are so strong, Cam…and determined to live.*

# DAY 3

## WAITING ROOM CHRONICLES

Nurse Inga called me first thing in the morning and said that your pressure had risen again through the night. The swelling in your face and head had become a challenge, so I was overwhelmingly concerned. However, by the time I'd arrived at the hospital, the medical team finally had been able to get your numbers under control. *What a relief!* The overall plan for the day was to keep you heavily sedated so that you could rest.

Before I could gather my thoughts and settle in by your bedside, my cell phone rang from an unidentified number. Under normal circumstances, I wouldn't have answered that type of call; however, the circumstances at the time were far from normal. I quickly answered with mixed emotions while I paced the empty ICU waiting room.

"Hello?" I answered.

"Good morning, Mrs. Daniels. This is Detective James from Prince George's County 4th Precinct. How are you this morning?"

"I could be better," I said sarcastically while sliding my back down the wall to sit on the floor. A chair just wouldn't do for *this* conversation. "Do you have any new information about who shot my son?"

"No, Ma'am. Not yet. But we are gathering some information as we speak. I first wanted to find out how Cameron was doing?"

I assumed the detective wanted to know if he was still collecting evidence for an attempted murder case that would possibly shift to a homicide investigation. With my face buried in the palm of my hand, I gave the detective a summarized, but diplomatic, response. "He continues to fight for his life, Detective James. He's currently heavily sedated, and the doctors are working to keep the pressure and swelling down in his head. They think that he will survive, but we're not 100% sure what's next for him. It's a waiting game right now."

"Well, it's good to hear that he is pulling through. I'm so sorry that you and your family are having to go through this, and we are going to do everything that we can to help. I was wondering if you had time to answer a few questions for me that may be helpful in your son's case. Is this a good time for you?"

"Sure."

The detective asked me all of the standard questions that did not seem helpful at all. *When's the last time I'd spoken to or seen you? Did I know who you were with that night? Did I know where you were going? Blah, Blah, Blah.* Any parent knew to ask *these* questions; and I'd already led this same interrogation with all your friends.

I was angry. I was angry with the people involved in hurting you. I was angry with the police for not making any arrests. I was angry at my ex-husband for not being present to take such a worthless call from the detective, leaving me alone to do it. And I was angry at myself for not being able to protect you.

After the detective collected all of the answers that I'm sure he'd already had, he assured me that he and his partner were working on the case and would be in touch with me soon. I rolled my eyes up in my head and let out a deep sigh as I stood up and headed for the ICU pods. For some reason, I didn't have much faith in Detective James. Maybe it was because of the countless unsolved shootings of young black men in our community, and the number of grieving mothers left with no justice. *But maybe, just maybe, your case would be different, Son,* I silently prayed as I entered your room.

When your father arrived at the hospital, we greeted each other with a hug just as we'd done the last two mornings, like the day before had never happened. I immediately began to download everything he'd missed since we last saw one another, including your medical updates and the phone call from the detective. There was no need to revisit nor rehash yesterday's events. I was over it and didn't suspect that it would happen again. We were both fully aware of the priority, so we picked up where necessary, and it was business as usual for our son. *Period.*

I peeked in on you many times throughout the day. However, I spent most of the morning in the waiting area completing the Family Medical Leave Act documents that I needed for work. FMLA is a federal labor law requiring covered employers to provide employees with job-protected, unpaid leave for qualified medical and family reasons. I certainly thought that my son suffering from a gunshot wound to the head qualified me for this coverage.

In calculating my leave-to date, I noted that I'd accumulated 7 weeks of vacation, 4 weeks of sick leave, and 5 days of personal leave...which totaled about 3 months of paid time off. According to the medical assessment provided, your recovery was estimated to extend to 12 months. *Oh well, I'll cross that bridge when I get to it,* I thought. At that moment, reporting to a job was the last thing on my mind. Thank God for a great organization that provided great benefits and peace of mind. In addition, I'd received a note from the union president to personally extend her thoughts and prayers to our family. Her sincere act of compassion really meant a lot to me.

Though everyone was genuinely concerned about your well-being, again, people could not help but wonder what had happened to you that night. Your brother was especially consumed with doing some investigative work with a couple of your friends, and together, they were able to provide some helpful information to the detectives. Social media and digital tracking are fascinating and can provide more information than most people realize. The kids were well-versed and able to connect the dots linking people, places, and things. That's why I'd always preach to my boys about being careful with what they said and did on social media outlets. The material is regulated and stored and can easily be accessed by the government whenever necessary. I prayed this technique would be used in helping to bring you some justice.

When I stepped out of the waiting room to stretch my legs, I walked up on a group of young men huddled in the hallway. I noticed the reduced volume of their voices when they saw me approaching. They were your friends, some of whom I knew personally and some not at all. One by one, they'd each had a chance to stand at your bedside to personally witness what gun violence had done to one of their friends. They all had a look of anger, sadness, and revenge in their eyes as they tried to discreetly glance over at me to be sure I hadn't heard any of their discussion. I was compelled to stand in the middle of this circle and look them in their eyes.

"Guys, thank you so much for being here to support Cameron. It means a lot to our family. But, LISTEN. If you all are even thinking about retaliating, please don't. I don't want to have to visit any of you at a trauma center...or worse. I understand your rage because believe me...I feel it, too. But please do not take the law into your own hands. The best way that you can help your friend right now is to contact me or David with any new information you learn about who did this, and we will pass it on to the authorities. And if you pray...pray!"

We all somberly promised one another that we would allow the police to do their jobs, and they each agreed to support their comrade in the way that I'd suggested. I hugged all of the boys tightly just as if they were my very own sons and wiped the tears that they so desperately tried to hide.

I scanned the room to acknowledge the number of familiar faces that had surfaced out of concern as the news about you continued to travel. I was pleasantly surprised at the level of support that so many people showed for our family. It was unbelievable. And during one of my many trips to the restroom that evening, I'd noticed Dex Brown talking with a group of people whom I didn't recognize. Coach Dex, as we affectionately called him, was once an athletic commissioner for the county youth program in which both you and David participated—for years! He must've heard about you and had come to the hospital to visit. I addressed him when I walked up on the group he was engaged with, "Hey Coach!" He looked surprised to see me, which immediately gave me pause. After we exchanged pleasantries, Coach Dex introduced me to his sisters and explained that his nephew had just been in a horrific car accident on the Baltimore-Washington Parkway. He'd been airlifted to the Trauma Center with a number of internal injuries and was fighting for his life. I felt that someone had punched me in the stomach all over again because I could barely speak from the lack of air in my body. I looked to Dex's sister, another unsettled mother, to console her of the grief I knew she was feeling. I gave her and Dex a brief summary of why I was also at the hospital, and we shared a moment of bonding that didn't require words. The Brown family joined us in the crowded waiting room that was filled with your visitors. They joined us in prayer and found a sense of comfort among the group.

Several of our friends and family members were present, although we'd discontinued visitation in your room. Again, everyone understood and most did not want to actually see you in your current state anyway. They were simply there to rally around us for support. My "Sista Circle" brought food, snacks, and beverages into the waiting room for the family. We passed around full bags of goodies to share among other visitors, while exchanging words of encouragement and needed laughs...probably a little too loudly and inappropriately for an ICU waiting room. I loved these ladies so much and appreciated their presence more than they knew.

Some of your visitors that day included Ronald, Scoop, Cindy, Michelle, Lameka, Ann N., Tashunda, Ann, Micaela, Carl, Dana, Wes, and Larry.

# DAY 4

## AN UNTRADITIONAL CELEBRATION OF LIFE

This day marked Granddaddy's 78th birthday. He was such an unselfish rock during that time being at the hospital all day, every day, greeting all of our visitors with hugs and smiles, and sitting in the very uncomfortable chairs in the waiting room for hours at a time. The last few days had aged him, but he did an excellent job pushing through such a trying time while keeping others lifted. It was a characteristic that I realized in my adult life I'd inherited from him. Fortunately, and unfortunately, pushing through trying times can be a gift and a curse. But he had truly been a gift to me during the most difficult time of my life.

My phone rang at 6 o'clock in the morning. It was Nurse Inga calling with a little excitement to her voice. I'd begun to connect with most of the nurses and establish relationships with them—especially the ones who were mothers. Inga told me that you had remained stable through the night, and your ICP number had remained low, under 15, nowhere near 30 where it had been days before. Only when she turned you over to change the pads on your bed did your number increase, but it immediately went back down. That was great news! We celebrated together over the phone for several seconds before I extended my sincere gratitude and disconnected the call.

While in route to the hospital, the head nurse on duty called me with a hematologist on the line. He told me that your blood was low; not alarmingly low, but you would definitely need a blood transfusion. You only needed one unit of blood, but the hospital legally had to obtain consent from me to begin the process. *JESUS!* My stomach was in knots, but I knew that my feedback would dictate what happened next in your recovery process. I gave the requested consent with a calm and confident response, although the knots had tightened and hurt 10 times worse. *Lord, please let this process go smoothly. Please let there be no negative reaction,* I prayed out loud.

I felt heavy. As I dragged through the halls of the hospital carrying bags of snacks, blankets, and electronics, I felt weak, tired, and sick. My immune system was diminishing. When I finally reached the common area of ICU right outside of the waiting room, I recognized two familiar faces. James Johnson and Willie Hope, who will always be known as *Slam-n-Jam's* "Coach James" and "Coach Willie," stood in the archway waiting to greet me. I hadn't seen either of these men in years, but they had come to show their support and love for you. Their presence immediately put a little spring in my step and a thankful smile on my face. Though we hadn't allowed many people to visit with you over the last couple of days, your father and I agreed to let the coaches see you. Your visitation was limited and restricted—but it just felt like the right thing to do.

Your father coached youth boys' basketball for a couple of years when you and David were really little. You were both always running around the gyms, chasing the older athletes, and stealing Gatorade from the coolers whenever you could. Once you were old enough, you both became instant athletes. Amateur Athletic Union (AAU) basketball was a huge part of our family life—if not most of it. We did it all: coaching, hosting tournaments, traveling, and even establishing a 501(c)(3) to single-handedly run our own nonprofit organization, *Star Youth Athletics.*

During that time of our lives, we were directly connected to hundreds of children, coaches, referees, families, and regional leaders of the industry. We definitely played an intricate role in the AAU rat race, and we loved every minute of it. It was a huge FAMILY that consisted of hundreds of people of all ages and walks of life. The adults formed personal relationships and created bonds with the children while watching them grow up right before our eyes, literally. Some of those associations still existed that day, which is why Coach James and Coach Willie were there...and why we allowed them to see you. We'd touched a lot of lives along the way, and there were several people from that world who still loved and cared for you.

Your father and I started to rotate sitting with you. One of us situated at your bedside to watch the machines, communicate with medical staff, and simply be close to you, while the other stayed in the ICU waiting room to receive the overwhelming number of visitors that came by to support us. I decided to sit with you during the early part of the day because, honestly, I just needed a little quiet time.

By mid-morning, I felt cold, tired, and achy. I hadn't had a menstrual cycle in many years, but I distinctly remember what cramps felt like. In that moment, not only was I experiencing the familiar feeling of PMS, but it also felt like my panties were soiled! I tried to ignore my physical discomfort and found solace in being still with you, along with the rhythmic beeping of the machines you were connected to. You slept, and so did I. I don't know how much time had elapsed before I was abruptly awakened by the blaring noise that reminded me of a high school fire drill.

I felt my face ball up. I was annoyed because my peaceful slumber had been interrupted. I stood up and looked closely at you, wondering if the loud honking would also disturb your rest. But thank goodness, you didn't budge. One of the ICU nurses stopped by your room and said quickly, but respectfully, "Ma'am, we're going to need you to step out and return to the waiting room until further notice, please." I looked at you, and you still had not flinched, so I gathered my things and prepared to leave your room.

Several medical staff ran by me, all heading toward Bed #8 three doors down from you. I walked in that direction because the doorway to exit the ICU was just beyond where several people were now huddled, including your assigned nurse. As I walked by the commotion, I could see that they were all trying to resuscitate a neighboring patient who needed emergency attention. The alarm continued to fill the room and sounded even louder with every step I took. My arms were full of chills as I finally found myself on the other side of the secured doors. I'd momentarily forgotten where I was. I'd just witnessed a Code Blue in the Trauma Center, and, unfortunately, the patient in Bed #8 wasn't as lucky as you.

I felt extremely sick—almost numb—and I just did not want to go back into the waiting room. I needed to make a trip to the ladies' room to try and settle my stomach and get a handle on this built-up anxiety. My nerves were all over the place. The bathroom was small and cold, but it was quiet. The largest stall wasn't spacious enough for all of my bags, so I took a risk of leaving them on the sink while I locked myself inside the toilet stall.

*Ugh! Why did I wear this romper today?* I needed to pull

down everything and expose my entire body in order to relieve myself. *What was I thinking when I put this thing on?* I sighed heavily and rolled my eyes.

As soon as I asked myself that question, I remembered why: the romper was the comfortable one-piece number that I'd snagged at the unforgettable *"Woman Evolve"* conference hosted by Sarah Jakes-Roberts in Denver, Colorado just the month before. I'd completed my last-minute registration just a week before the event, found the most inexpensive flight on an unfamiliar airline, and planned the journey with my co-worker/sister-friend Lameka and her sister-in-love, Dora. None of us knew what to expect and had no idea what a roller coaster ride we were in store for.

Satan apparently did not want us to be there because he surely put obstacle after obstacle after obstacle in our path, hoping that we'd give up and return home. Our flight was delayed without notice and later canceled just moments before take-off, and our rental car reservation was non-existent once we were finally on the ground.

*BUT GOD!*

From the start of the actual conference to the very end, we each were inspired and equipped with nuggets of life lessons and memorable gifts to bring back home...including the romper!

*What the...?* I noticed a familiar red hue in the lining of my panties. I hadn't seen blood in that area in over six years! *What in the world is going on?* I wondered.

I created an old-school, makeshift sanitary napkin with a wad of toilet paper and wondered why I was now having my period. *This is all I need,* I thought as my eyes welled up with tears.

*NOTE TO SELF: Call your doctor to make an appointment.*

I carefully reassembled my clothes, and slowly wiped, flushed, and stepped out of the stall. I was still alone in the bathroom, and my bags were still on the sink. *Thank goodness.* As I washed my hands, the mirror's reflection looked as if all the melanin had left my face. I looked drained, tired, and sickly. But…I picked up my bags, took a deep breath, and flung open the ladies' room door—somehow, as strong as ever.

Your cousin Marty had arrived in town, so he accompanied your father during his shift to sit with you. The medical staff told us a couple of days ago that even though you were sedated, you could sense the presence of people and activity around you, and you could definitely hear. Even though your father was trying to whisper, his voice was as deep, loud, and distinct as usual. His and Marty's booming voices together caused you to surprisingly open your eyes! You weren't 100% coherent, and your eyes weren't focused on anything in particular, but the sound of familiar voices definitely got your attention and a positive reaction. It was a baby step, but progress in the right direction, and we celebrated the small success!

Grandmama came into town later that afternoon from Florida, and she made her way straight to the hospital to see you. Among other visitors were Aunt Pat and her Usher Board friends, Terry, Kim, Butch, Damon, Lameka, Coach Phil and Ms. Peggy, Mike and Rhonda, Wendy, LaShawn, Ms. Mo, Lil Calvin, Kristin, Dana and her husband, Cindy, and Uncle Kevin.

Once again, people brought bags of food, boxes of

snacks, and packages of water for us to have available in the waiting room for our family and visitors. We'd spent long days there, and the hospital had become our second home. We were surrounded by so much love and support with each passing hour, and it definitely made the very difficult time a little easier.

When we prepared to leave you for the evening and tell you good night, the nurses had already changed shifts. I didn't recognize the staff person covering your night assignment. He seemed uninterested, unenthused, and unengaged. *We're going to have to break him in and show him the ropes!* He was unfamiliar with you and had to get to know you as a new patient…and us as a new family. We exchanged introductions and pleasantries, and Nurse Bill told us that they were scheduling you for a contrast scan the next day to look at the blood vessels in your brain and main cavity. Hopefully this would determine if there was any extensive damage done to your nervous system.

I had trouble resting and sleeping that night. David had gone back to Baltimore, and I was staying in my house for the first time since you'd been gone. Against Tom's recommendation, I'd decided to return home, despite my feelings of anxiety and fear. Until then, I'd constantly been surrounded by people for the last four days, and I just wanted to lay in my own bed to be alone with my own thoughts.

I couldn't help but constantly be reminded that the police weren't any closer to making an arrest and that an attempted murderer continued to walk the streets. *Did he know that you survived his malicious crime? And if so, would he come to our home to send a message by attempting another heinous act on me?* I'd be ready for him, one way or the other. But despite my confidence and preparedness, my overacting nerves were still in control. I cried for the majority of the night, unsure of how to settle myself, and unsure if I even wanted to. I just missed you so much and as promised, I'd left the light on in the foyer for you.

*NOTE TO SELF: Research home security cameras.*

# DAY 5

## SO FAR, SO GOOD

Bill did not voluntarily call me first thing that morning like the other night nurses had done, even though I'd verified my cell phone number with him and asked him to do so before I left the hospital. Therefore, I called him. Again, he gave very little emotion in his dry report about you, if that's what you want to call it. "Uneventful. He rested well through the night," was all the nurse offered. *Oh, Bill. Tsk, tsk, tsk. Just wait 'til I see you again,* I warned him in my head.

I arrived at the hospital fairly early. The waiting room was chillier than usual, and I was the first visitor to arrive. I claimed our favorite set of chairs in the back corner, which allowed me to see the entire room.

There was a square table next to our section that normally housed magazines and other reading materials for visitors. However, we had cleared it off days ago and used it to hold bags of snacks, lay out food, and store bottles of juice and water.

After I checked in on you and talked to your day nurse, I stepped out of the room as they prepared you for the contrast scan. I'd planned to hang around the ICU pod for the duration of the short procedure. While I waited, I'd noticed the monitors that hung above each patient's doorway, listing vitals and other important information for the nursing staff to clearly view.

I'd been familiarizing myself with all the numbers, acronyms, and graphs over the last several days, so when I glanced over at your immediate neighbor's monitor, I recognized the displayed data. He was the person who had been admitted during the same night you were and appeared to be in a coma. Sadly, he still had not been identified by anyone, and the blinking screen above his door read "Nevada Doe." My heart ached for him, a complete stranger, and I felt helpless. Then it hit me! What must the number of unidentified people in a hospital look like? Some have families, and some do not have anyone. And the method that Prince George's Hospital Center used to organize these statistics was to customize each John Doe with the name of a city or state...because the numbers must be that great.

All I could think to do in that moment was simply return to the waiting room and sit still for a while. So, that's what I did, hoping to have a little time to myself to reflect. But before long, visitors slowly began to trickle in and join me in our reserved corner.

Your Nana, David, Makeba, and my colleague Valencia were all sitting with me that morning when Bishop Marcell Crawford came into the waiting room. Bishop Crawford was a minister at Kingdom Life, and he and another Hospital Chaplain were making their rounds to talk to visiting family members. When they made their way back to our corner of the waiting room, I told them that I was visiting my son and I asked if they would pray with us. Both of the ministers humbly and eagerly obliged. We all stood and joined hands to form a small circle, and Brother Crawford belted out a powerful prayer, almost like he knew us and the details of your story. He asked if it was okay to visit your bedside and pray over you, and I agreed.

Once Brother Crawford returned to the waiting room, he shared his own story with us. He explained that he had been shot in the eye 35 years ago and had made a full recovery. Looking at and listening to him, one would never know his challenges. He said that you reminded him so much of himself, and he assured us that you'd be okay too. *Wow. What a morning!*

The day just continued to get better! The doctors were able to remove one of the two drainage tubes from your head because your bleeding had slowed tremendously. And soon afterward, the metal monitor on your head that measured the pressure on your brain was removed. Your ICP levels had remained in the normal range for two days, so the medical team felt like it was time to safely remove it.

When they took you off the Propofol sedative later that morning, you began moving a lot and opening your eyes. You responded to commands, gave a thumbs up, and even squeezed everyone's hands. But you soon became overly excited and seemingly irritated, probably trying to figure out where you were and what was going on. You squirmed around so much that you wore yourself out, and the nurse decided to put you back on the sedative to calm you down.

At that point, your father and I agreed with the doctors to discontinue your visitation for the day. Only immediate family would be allowed to see you. Your blood pressure had spiked again from all the activity and anxiety, I supposed. I spoke to you gently and held your hand in an attempt to help relax you.

"You're doing great, Cam. You are so strong. And I'm right here with you, kid. Hang in there. Everything is going to be okay."

A single tear escaped your closed eye lid and rolled down the side of your face as you tightly squeezed my hand. You heard me and knew exactly who I was just by the sound of my voice. I knew you were scared, so it took everything in me not to cry or allow my voice to crack. You needed my strength, and both your brain and body needed to heal. *Rest, baby. Rest.*

Though none of your visitors today could actually see you, the waiting room remained packed! Probably breaking the rules, we cleared off the top of the credenza that extended across the back of the waiting room wall. I placed the magazines, boxes, and office supplies inside the empty drawers to make space for all of the food that people had brought in.

My Team Logistics sister, Jen, brought in some healthy, but heavy Mediterranean hors d'oeuvres from her favorite neighborhood store, while MJ brought in a full-blown chicken feast with an array of side dishes from Sardi's. A family-sized bucket of fried chicken showed up, with biscuits, french fries, green beans, mashed potatoes, and gravy; and Valencia later returned with dinner-sized containers of baked turkey wings, sweet potatoes, and greens.

We'd turned the ICU credenza into a family buffet! Laughs and loud chatter filled the room as people fixed plates, ate, and kept our family company. This very unique gathering also consisted of Kenny, Coach Phil, Uncle Dee, Tammy and Natalia, Makeba, Leah and Derek, Moody, Tim, Nick, Maceo, Angel, Domonique, Stephanie, Kisha and Adrian, JaJa, Nita, and several of your teammates from your high school baseball squad. Words simply could not describe the heartfelt scene of community in that waiting room.

# DAY 6

## FROM TOO MUCH INFO…TO NO INFO

My doctor's office was able to work me in for an appointment first thing in the morning, so I made a stop there on my way to the hospital. Luckily, it was en route. I was still bleeding, but not as heavily, thank God. I couldn't remember the last time I'd purchased sanitary napkins or panty liners, and the constant presence of one between my legs just felt weird. I was tired and my energy was low, so I knew that my iron level had decreased from the loss of blood.

Unfortunately, the doctor that I'd been seeing for the last 15 years was on summer vacation. *Just my luck!* I hated having to explain my entire medical history to a new physician. I didn't have time for all the questions…I needed to get to the hospital. *Please lady, enough with the interrogation, already!*

With my feet pressed against the cold stirrups, and my eyes rolled up in my head with annoyance, I continued to answer what seemed liked useless questions. It seemed to take forever for "Dr. Whatever-Her-Name-Is" to finally look under my gown to confirm that all of the answers I provided were true: *No, I don't have a uterus; No, I don't have a cervix; And yes, I'm bleeding!*

But it wasn't until I burst into tears of frustration and blurted out, "My son has been shot…in the head…and I'm trying to hurry this appointment along so I can get to the hospital!" The room became so quiet that we both could hear a pin drop. "Dr. What's-Her-Name" looked stunned, and she had no idea how to respond to my emotional outburst. Finally, in her attempt to console me, she offered her deepest apologies before determining that my diagnosis was a sure case of stress. My mind and body had been experiencing emotional and physical trauma, and I needed to try to stay off my feet as much as possible and rest. *Easier said than done,* I thought. I wondered if she was a mother of a Black son too, and if she sincerely felt my pain. She extended some much-needed words of encouragement, and then in her next breath, she offered me a prescription for a yeast infection and asked me to get dressed as she left the room. *Well damn. What just happened?*

*NOTE TO SELF: When I pick up my prescription, remember to also grab some vitamins to help strengthen my immune system.*

By the time I finally arrived at the hospital, your father was already there, along with a few visitors. Two people from my employer's leadership team had stopped by to visit, and I appreciated them taking time from their busy schedules to show their support to my family. It meant a lot. Though they asked what they could do to help, I honestly did not have that answer. I think I was, to some extent, still in shock myself, and my brain hadn't quite settled down enough to think about what our needs were. We were just really starting to feel confident that you would survive, but we were still unsure of what to expect in your recovery process. Once things were clearer, I'd hoped to go back to the leadership team to take them up on the offer to help us.

More visitors continued to fill the waiting room later that day: Shaune and Deja, Dave, Dora, LeAnn, Tammy and Natalia, Uncle Dee, Kisha, Nana and Granddaddy, Micaela, Lameka and Dorjan, Racine and Mark. But little did we know, the warm and fuzzy feel of the waiting room would soon all change. Because you were a gunshot victim with a pending investigation, we were forced to have a tough conversation with the hospital's Head of Security.

The same nervousness and anxiety I felt when I was at home alone had followed me to the hospital. There were so many people showing up to the hospital asking for you, I became concerned for your safety. There was no sign-in process at the front desk, no request to show identification, and no security check before visitors were immediately directed to ICU. If people whom we *knew* showed up unexpectedly, who's to say that people whom we *did not know* wouldn't show up as well? What if someone who'd heard that you had survived was still looking for you? What if someone wanted to do you additional harm? What if someone showed up who was willing to hurt your family members or innocent visitors? How could we protect our son and prevent this from potentially happening?

After discussing the possible risks with the Head of Security, unfortunately, your father and I made the difficult decision to put you on the "NO INFO" list, which meant your name would no longer be listed publicly on the hospital's registry. And we could no longer have visitors outside of our five immediate family members. *That sucked!* But, you couldn't protect yourself, so it was my responsibility to do what was best for you. Therefore, as of the start of visiting hours the next day, the once-packed ICU waiting room would be no more.

# DAY 7

## #CAMSTRONG EMERGES!

I woke up feeling more somber than I had the last few days. You were making progress with each passing day, which was a blessing. But I knew I'd miss the smiling faces and distracting chatter in the waiting room. However, I continued with my routine of packing a hefty bag of snacks and beverages that so many visitors had brought to us over the last week. The five of us on your visitors' list would never be hungry while at the hospital.

On my way to you, I made a pit stop at my dentist's office to have the much-awaited permanent cap quickly installed over my front tooth. At least I'd hoped that it would be a quick process. But sure enough, the visit was anything but simple.

Just a month prior at a routine check-up, I'd let the dentist talk me into finally replacing the tooth that became damaged over time from a root canal. I'd been fitted for a shiny new porcelain fixture, and since then, had been extremely careful with my eating while wearing a raggedy, temporary look-alike. If anyone had looked closely enough, they would've surely seen the plastic discrepancy. Just two weeks later, the fake make-shift tooth had fallen out after I'd taken an inappropriate bite from a slice of pepperoni pizza, and the dentist glued it back into my head during an emergency visit. The adjustment had been quite frustrating, and almost unbearable to deal with while I worried about your recovery. Therefore, when the dentist's office called to inform me that my replacement was ready, I was anxious to finally have it fixed. And this was the only time I had to do it.

As I lay in the plush chair and waited longer than I should have, I began to hear the dental assistants blame each other for being unable to locate my tooth. I'm sure one of them heard my overly exaggerated deep sigh because she poked her head in the room and with a fake, calm tone said, "I'll be right with you." *Great, this is all I need,* I thought as I rubbed my temples.

I had no idea when I would have time to go back if the dental staff could not find my replacement during that visit. When I closed my eyes in frustration, all I could see was your face, and tears began to stream down both sides of my own. Time seemed to stand still. I could hear my heart rapidly beating so hard, and my chest actually ached from the pounding. *I'm out of here,* I decided. Just as I was about to get up and leave, the dentist and her assistant rushed into the room, excited to bring in the tooth they'd just found.

Rolling and wiping my eyes at the same time, I couldn't help but unleash the rant that those ladies probably did not deserve. "Why would you call me and say that my tooth was ready if you had no idea where it was?" I chastised. "This is so unprofessional and a total inconvenience to me. My son is fighting for his life right now, and I've been in here for 30 minutes, waiting on you all to find a tooth that you called ME to say you had. Please hurry up so I can get to the hospital!" The tears continued to flow while I displayed the "ugly cry," and my voice trembled with each escalated octave.

The two women froze in their tracks and looked like deer caught in the headlights. The dentist broke several moments of silence when she finally found the words to apologize for the mix-up and express condolences for my family's situation. I knew that she had not wanted to pry, but her curiosity had eventually gotten the best of her when she asked, "What happened to your son, if you don't mind me asking?"

I managed to answer clearly with a firm voice, "My son was mugged. He was shot in the head and left for dead a week ago, but he is fighting really hard to pull through."

The ladies turned into mannequins once again and were both at a loss for words.

"So, the sooner we can finish up here, the sooner I can get to the hospital," I added.

The dentist probably installed my new fixture in record time, because before I knew it, I was looking at my reflection in the handheld mirror that her assistant had shoved in my face. The new tooth looked great, but the bags under my eyes, the wrinkles on my forehead, and my scaly, unkempt skin all caused me to quickly put the mirror down in disgust.

Though the ladies could only imagine my pain and surely excused my rude behavior, I apologized for my outburst before I thanked them and hurried out of the front door. I was sorry. Well, not sorry, but definitely late.

Your father, brother, grandparents, and I were the only people permitted to see you. And in order to obtain a visitor's badge at the front desk, we were each required to give a secret password to the attending security guard upon entrance. "Celtics." Your favorite team that wears your favorite color.

Daryl and Jasper were your nurses for the day, two young men with whom I was very impressed. They told me that your blood pressure had been high overnight, so the goal that day was to work on keeping it stabilized. They gave you a diuretic to relieve the puffiness in your hands, which was caused by all the fluids pumped into your body intravenously. Your medical team had also decided to take the second drainage tube out of your head because your bleeding had subsided significantly.

Unfortunately, there was a new problem. You had developed acute respiratory distress syndrome. In other words, PNEUMONIA! X-rays had clearly identified the fluid build-up in your left lung, so the staff began treating it immediately. A respiratory therapist, who would use various techniques to physically move the secretions around, was scheduled to see you regularly.

The therapist would turn you on your side while she literally beat your back to help loosen the blockage. She would rotate the process of using her hands and using a huge suction cup-like apparatus. You were given antibiotics through your IV, and the doctors used a special catheter to suck the secretions out of your lungs since you could not cough it up on your own. What a grueling process, and it was so very hard to watch! You'd been ordered a special bed that would massage your back and help move and break up the stubborn fluids, but it would take a while for it to arrive.

I needed a break to recharge and restore my faith, so I decided to sit in the waiting room and check the many texts and voicemails left on my cell phone. God sent me the timely distractions that I needed, without a doubt.

Though I tried to notify as many people as possible last night, some visitors had arrived at the hospital, only to be told that you were not a patient listed on the registry. People were frantic and confused at the news, resulting in a number of missed calls and unanswered texts while I dealt with the latest news of your medical issue.

My former supervisor, Dorothy, had waited in the main lobby of the hospital until she heard from and laid eyes on me. It was great to see her, and her positive energy was exactly what I needed at that time. She came armed with bags of food, and a batch of her favorite shea butter to use as I saw fit. I thanked Dorothy as I walked her out the front doors of the hospital to then meet Makeba, who'd just pulled up on two wheels to hand off a family-sized bag of Subway sandwiches and chips from the girls. *Lunch!* The timing was perfect! Then I received a call from Larry, who was in the lobby with a pan of his homemade lasagna. *More food!*

I had missed several calls and texts from Belinda throughout the day, but later, I was finally able to catch my breath to answer. She and Derwinn both knew that we could no longer have visitors, but they asked that I meet them in the main lobby of the hospital.

*Deep sigh. Not more food,* I thought. As drained as I was—physically and emotionally—I once again took the lengthy walk from the Trauma Center to the hospital entrance, and my feet and legs felt as if I'd walked 10 miles by then. The pair greeted me with hugs and apologized for the disturbance, promising to not keep me away from your bedside long. They explained how they'd thought long and hard on how to lead our Largo High School Class of '89 in an organized effort of support for our family without creating a GoFundMe Page, which I hated and profusely opposed. Then they proceeded to present me with customized T-shirts in your favorite green color that read #*CamStrong* across the front, matching the silicone wrist bands that I'd already ordered and planned to distribute. There was a T-shirt for each member of our immediate family. I was speechless.

The idea was to make the paraphernalia available at a cost, and part of the proceeds would go towards any lingering medical expenses. This was a perfect campaign that allowed people to be supportive silently, while creating a bold message of unity during your recovery. Words simply could not express how appreciative I was of the thought behind this gesture, as well as the symbol of strength this would later become. *My class is better than yours!*

You rested throughout the day, but by nightfall, your blood pressure was sky-high again. The medical team tried to successfully manage it, but it was most likely a result of the infection in your lungs and your continued pain. They decided to give you a different medication to manage the fluctuation, but your body was very slow to respond to it. The maximum dosage of pain medication was 200mg, from which you'd been reduced to 150mg earlier in the day. However, with the increase in your blood pressure, compiled with the pneumonia, the doctors decided to revisit the maximum dosage in order to keep you comfortable.

That day had been a rough one. You'd taken one step forward, then three steps back. But I'd continued to pray over you and cover your body in anointed oil. It was hard to leave your bedside that night, but I knew that in order to be strong for you, I needed to take care of myself.

Before I lay down for the night around midnight, I called your night nurse to check on you. Alvina was happy to tell me that your blood pressure had begun to decrease. It seemed that you had been in extreme pain that evening, but you just could not tell us.

"Stay strong, Cam," I said as I hung up. "You are such a fighter."

*#CamStrong*

# DAY 8

## IF I COULD TAKE AWAY YOUR PAIN

I woke up startled by a 5 a.m. call from the hospital. Nurse Alvina said that you were doing well; no episodes during the night, and your blood pressure had remained in place. Your special massage bed had not arrived yet, but the respiratory therapist was still administering her techniques on you. You'd had a good night, and your nurse just wanted to let me know that before she'd ended her shift. I really appreciated the special thought and effort that some of the nurses put into their jobs. It truly made a difference during a very unsettling process.

I arrived at the hospital during my usual morning hour before anyone else from your limited visitors' list. Dr. Hobbs, the attending physician on duty, informed me that the plan for the day was to slowly decrease your sedation, while keeping you as comfortable as possible. "So far, so good," she advised. "He's a little groggy this morning, but he's making good progress and moving in the right direction."

I looked over at you as the doctor gave her update, and you lay very still and calm as you stared off into space. Dr. Hobbs gave you a couple of standard commands and you followed them well. "Good morning, Cam. You're doing so great, Son," I praised you as the doctor exited your room; and you squeezed my hand as tightly as you could to signify that you'd taken in my words of affirmation. *Thank God!*

Surprisingly, you then waved your right hand… the only mobile one… to flag down a nurse who was passing by the doorway. You could apparently see fairly well through your squinted eyes...and at a decent distance! The passing nurse acknowledged you and quickly came into the room. She leaned in close to you, held your hand, and asked you a barrage of questions to determine what you needed her to do. It took her several guesses to figure out what you wanted. Finally, when she mentioned the wedge-like pillows that were tucked under your side, you squeezed her hand. You were uncomfortable and wanted them removed from your bed. The nurses routinely shifted the wedges from one side of your body to the other to prevent bed sores and ulcers by not allowing you to lie flat on your back. Judging by the strength you used to squeeze the nurse's hand, you wanted to be laid down on your back immediately. You would always manage to get your point across one way or another.

When the respiratory therapist showed up to work on you, she gave you what looked like the old breathing treatment that we used to give you for your asthma when you were a little boy. But with the nebulizer she used, a prescribed medication was not put into the reservoir...only saline. Using salt water helped you breathe better by moisturizing your airway. And this process would move around the thick mucus that would in turn be sucked out by a specialized catheter.

Later in the day, Granddaddy and Nana visited with you. Your relationship with them always made you feel loved and safe, and they definitely had been your unspoken security blanket throughout your entire life. They treated these moments no differently, as they each spoke softly to you, assuring you that everything would be okay. Nana held your hand while you appeared to look beyond her with unawareness, and Granddaddy read a sports article to you from the daily newspaper. Grandparents always seem to know exactly what to do.

After an hour or so, they told you that they were going to leave and allow you to rest, but they promised to come back the next day. Hearing that, you became visibly upset and agitated, and you began to cry. As strong as your Nana is, she couldn't bear to see you in such duress, so she left the room as she also started cry. When your Granddaddy walked out behind her, you threw a good old-fashioned temper tantrum, which caused all the machines to beep loudly in place of the screams that you were unable to belt out on your own. You broke out in a massive sweat that covered your entire face. The episode caused your blood pressure to rise at a concerning all-time high, and the nurses scrambled to calm you...all because you did not want to see your grandparents go.

After being sedated, you finally calmed down and fell asleep. I sat at your bedside and just watched you rest for a while. Maybe you felt my presence because you suddenly woke up from your slumber and started agonizing about something. I called your nurse in, and it looked like you were trying to talk and tell us something. You were crying, squirming, and frantically pulling at whatever you could get your hand on.

"Cam, I'm here, baby. It's okay. Settle down," I repeated softly, rubbing your moving hand. But I could not soothe you, and neither could the nurse. Something was wrong. Perhaps you had awakened with the last memory of your grandparents leaving the room. Maybe you were having a flashback of the moments before being shot. I felt helpless because I didn't know how to help you. I wished I could read your mind; or better yet...I wished I could simply trade places with you. The nurses asked me to step out of your room so they could get you settled. They put the maximum dosage of pain medication directly into your IV, which immediately sedated you again. That seemed to be the only way to keep you calm and allow you to rest for the remainder of the evening.

One day at a time, and one step at a time.

*#CamStrong*

# DAY 9

## NOT JUST ANOTHER STATISTIC

Whenever Bill was assigned as your night nurse, he never gave me a courtesy call in the mornings with an update on you like his colleagues did. Therefore, I called him at 7:45 a.m. before he finished his shift. He plainly told me that you had no issues during the night, and your vitals had remained stable. *You're doing good, Cam. You just need to rest…and heal.* Unfortunately, the special bed that would help with moving around the secretions in your body still had not arrived. Until then, the respiratory therapist would continue to work on you regularly.

With the new "NO INFO" policy in place, the handful of us sat in the waiting room together while you rested. We all wore our green *#CamStrong* T-shirts that my classmates had made for us, which got much attention from staff and other visitors. We took commemorative group pictures in the waiting area that would later be used for announcements, posts, and other communication around your health and recovery.

David and your father sat at your bedside for a while. They read current events news articles to you to keep you abreast on what was happening in the world, while also sharing updates from the sports section. Your brother held your hand and gave you the latest news from the music world. You continued to respond to commands, squeezing everyone's hands and giving a thumbs up or down to answer questions. You had this form of communication down to a tee. When I later sat with you, I talked to you about all the visitors who had come by to visit, and all the nice gestures that people had extended over the last several days. I described the many greeting cards that outlined the walls of your room, and the many balloons that were now beginning to lose some of their helium. When I told you about the *#CamStrong* theme that had emerged in your honor, you squeezed my hand so tightly that it actually hurt. I grimaced but wouldn't dare tell you that I was in pain. I was just glad to know that your strength was intact, and apparently, so were your emotions.

While I was with you, Dr. Hobbs ironically made her rounds again. I'd just met her the day before, and it was rare to run into the same covering doctor so soon. *But God!* Before she could even begin talking, I invited her to step outside of your room to semi-privately speak with her. As your mother and advocate, I felt compelled to humanize your existence, your survival, your LIFE. The other day, several residents had followed her and hung on her every word as she stopped at each bed to visit all the ICU patients. As she stood over you to tell me about your status, she strangely said with pride that "they weren't expecting you to make it." I think I was in shock and simply at a loss of words at the time. It wasn't until she left the room that it hit me, and my eyebrow lifted with discomfort. *How insensitive could she be? Why would she say that, standing right over a patient, when he is clearly conscious and can hear everything?* There was no compassion for how that made you feel, nor me. But somehow, I suppose doctors feel a sense of gratification from seeing a patient go from a potential "lost cause" to "a miracle." They get the credit and satisfaction of feeling like they saved someone, so it becomes the proud part of the report to say that they changed the statistic of the rising number of Black kids who lost their lives to gun violence...today, anyway. *Meh.* It was nothing to her and meant nothing to allow that comment to roll off her tongue so nonchalantly. Luckily, I was given the opportunity to tell her just how that made OUR family feel, as I'm confident she's made other families feel before us. I told her to never do that again with my son. Even though she may not have agreed with my theory, she respected my wishes, which is all I wanted. Maybe she'll keep my face and my words in mind the next time she is in this situation, addressing a grieving mother. And sadly, there will be a next time.

The Hospital Chaplain, Bishop Crawford, stopped by your room to visit today. He held our hands and prayed, offering us encouraging words and powerful uplift. The Bishop was excited about how much progress you'd made since the last time he'd seen you and was very much interested in hearing the positive updates. He told us that he would be out of town for a week, starting tomorrow, but wanted to check in on you before leaving. He promised to continue to pray for you, and as soon as he returned to the city, he'd be back to visit.

Daryl and Jasper became two of our favorite nurses. They were so attentive and very calming. They each had gone above and beyond to make sure you rested comfortably and that your vitals continued to remain stable. Daryl recommended that I begin recording and tracking your many medications each day. For information and reference, he printed a full list of your current medications, along with the dosages, and I could not even begin to thank him enough for it. I'd just been keeping everything in my overworked memory bank over the last several days, so this gesture definitely helped to replenish a little of my mental space:

*Enoxaparin (Lovenox)* – blood thinner
*Guaifenesin* – secretions in your chest
*Metoclopronide (Reglan)* – ulcers
*Propranolol (Inderal)* – blood pressure

*Oxycodone* - pain
*Fentanyl* - sedative

At 19 years old, you were having to endure unspeakable things. Gunshot wound, brain surgery, temporary paralysis, pneumonia, severe pain, and a medicine cabinet full of narcotics. And sadly, that was only the beginning.

# DAY 10

## JUST A LIONESS AND HER CUB

Though your father had relocated to another city just weeks before you were shot, your unexpected medical emergency would not allow him to stay there. In my opinion, you were at a stage of life where you desperately needed your father in your life anyway, whether or not either of you chose to admit it. But the separation and recent divorce affected you differently than they did your brother, and it would've been nice if you had more hands-on attention from a male figure.

God definitely takes drastic measures sometimes to answer prayers because your father started out on an early morning drive to the tri-state area to pack up his new swanky apartment and return home.

David left for Baltimore to prepare for the upcoming college semester. I knew I'd be alone with you at the hospital, with very little breaks and no shift changes. I was up for it though, and I armored myself as necessary.

When I felt myself wake up, I kept my eyes closed and stayed curled up in the fetal position, which had become a new norm for me.

I began to pray, asking God to continue healing you. I prayed that you would be peaceful and trust God enough to rely on Him to bring you comfort. I thanked the Lord for the outpouring of support from friends and family. And I asked Him to give me the extra courage and patience to endure the day alone with you in the hospital. I knew that there was only one source to conjure up the unimaginable strength that I needed to get through the day…and the days to come. I had to dig deep down in my faith, even when I thought I'd lost it.

I called Nurse Bill around 7:30 a.m., and once again he told me that your night was "uneventful." You remained stable all night with no changes, and all your vitals were good. Unfortunately, he said that the special bed that had been ordered a few days ago still had not been delivered, which was becoming discouraging.

When I arrived at your hospital room later in the morning, there were no nurses sitting outside of your room monitoring you. Over the last several days, I'd successfully learned how to read the beeping machines that you were connected to, and I understood exactly what each number meant. Your blood pressure was at almost 200, and I freaked the hell out!

I stormed out of your room and loudly demanded to know who was assigned to Bed #5, as your whiteboard had not been updated with any new information. A nurse ran out of one of the adjacent rooms to assist me, and she quickly looked up the requested information, throwing "Nurse Terri" under the bus. She frantically explained that your new nurse had taken another patient to the operating room but would return shortly. So, until then, you unfortunately had to lie there, probably in pain, while your machines beeped. You were visibly sweating, and if one looked closely enough, they could probably see smoke coming from *both* of our ears. I was furious as I fanned you with a stack of random papers that I grabbed from the table, and I adjusted your blankets to try to give you some temporary relief.

Though Terri probably arrived within the next few minutes, it felt like a lifetime. Sharp sarcasm and a few curse words sat on the tip of my tongue. The personal angel that lived on one shoulder battled with the miniature devil that frequently showed up on the other. Instead of blurting out the first thing that came to mind as Terri crossed the threshold of your room, I just gave her a look that probably made her want to immediately turn around and go home for the day…even though she'd just started her shift. But your new nurse was brave. I'm sure she's felt the wrath of many mothers throughout her career, so she was ready for me. She officially introduced herself while she simultaneously checked the beeping machines and muted them. Then she smiled and told me that she had good news.

You were officially out of the "critical condition" status and updated to "serious." But because of that, your nurses would now be assigned to TWO patients, as opposed to just you.

*Wait…Did she just play the Jedi Mind Trick on me?* I wasn't exactly sure how to feel about what Terri said or how to even respond. I was stuck, which does not happen often. She continued by sharing with me that during the night shift, your heart rate had dropped. The night nurse could not administer your scheduled dose of blood pressure medication because it would've caused your heart rate to plummet out of control. Therefore, you had to skip last night's manual dosage, which was why your blood pressure was so high and your machines were going crazy. Bill had flat out lied, and Terri was my new ally for the day.

You simply did not feel well. You continued to be agitated and fretful throughout most of the day, which was very concerning. Though Terri had another patient, I wore her out, and we had an unspoken understanding that YOU were the priority. Whenever I called, she made herself available immediately. She and the other nurses consulted with the on-call doctors for resolution to make you comfortable. Finally, they decided to put you back on the IV drip for blood pressure medication that would make an immediate and steady difference. That finally worked. *Thank God!*

You were settling down, so I decided to gather my things and sit out in the waiting room to allow you to rest peacefully. I needed to look at a different set of walls myself. Nana and Granddaddy came by to sit with me for a while and keep me company but also decided not to disturb you. And later, LeAnn stopped by the hospital to drop off some timely dinner to me at the front entrance.

A different respiratory therapist worked on you this evening...Vicky. She was a middle-aged Black woman, and I noticed the tenderness that she applied to her technique. When she talked to you, her soft tone and careful instructions were very personable. I liked the way she handled you, even though she had to use stern hands to help move the mucus through your lungs. There was a certain motherly touch that she had that only another mother could recognize. You felt it, too.

You felt safe and loved as Vicky gently flipped you from one side to the other and beat on your back. She thoroughly explained her techniques to you, but periodically, she directed her eyes at me. She also took the time to describe the functions of the breathing machine that you were hooked up to and showed me what the numbers meant. You were breathing a lot on your own, but the goal was to lessen the percentage that you relied on the machine each day. Vicky saw the fear and nervousness in my eyes. She said, "Mom, this is YOUR baby. Don't be afraid to touch him. You can take care of your child, just like you would normally do. Massage his feet and hands with lotion to keep his skin moist. And what kind of music does he like? It should be okay for you to bring in a radio for him now. He's out of the woods."

This lady did not know what her kind actions and words meant for me that evening. She was exactly what I prayed for that morning, and God didn't let me down. I got the extra oomph that I needed to keep me going. *Thank you, Lord. I will definitely begin doing these things for my son tomorrow.*

# DAY 11

## LIFE ALWAYS FINDS A WAY

I woke up earlier than normal for some reason. I felt like it was going to be a good day. I was feeling more confident in "mothering" you, and I was looking forward to personally connecting with you again. I couldn't wait for the call from your night nurse, so I called Ricky myself at 7:00 a.m. to check in on you. He said that you had a good night with no issues. All your vitals had remained stable with no spikes in your blood pressure. *Good news!*

After showering and putting on some loose-fitting clothes, I packed the usual snacks and beverages in my red and white over-sized Costco bag. This had become the regimen that I followed every day like clockwork, and I could probably now do it with my eyes closed. I had been on autopilot for the last several days. But this particular day felt different when I packed my portable fan, a wireless speaker, and the shea butter that Dorothy had given me. *THIS* was going to be a good day on purpose. A better day!

When I walked into your room this morning, you were awake! They had taken you off the sedatives, and TODAY'S GOAL written on your white board was to take you off the ventilator! This was major.

You were moving quite a bit, like a baby discovering his limbs for the first time. You especially stretched out your feet and legs, probably wondering what was weighing them down. Because you had been lying dormant for so long, it was necessary for you to wear compression boots on your feet that not only kept your ankles erect, but also helped with your blood circulation. There was definitely nothing wrong with your legs. They looked extra-long and lanky with each kick. I was excited to see such movement, and you squeezed my hand when you heard me cheering for you.

You still could not move your left hand and arm, which were both really swollen. You were much calmer than you were the day before but frustrated because you didn't have full mobility of your body. Though your eyes were open, they wandered off into space, unable to focus on anything. But I stood on the right side of your body because it was the direction in which you appeared to stare. Also, your right arm was the limb that desperately followed my voice to feel my back and pull me in for an attempted hug.

I softly explained to you that I was wearing the bracelet that was in your room, the stretchy one with the crosses...black, white, and pink. I awaited your reaction to determine if you'd remember, and if so, how would you tell me. With your strong fingers, you blindly felt up my arm until you could actually feel the bracelet, tugging on it so hard to confirm that I thought it was going to break.

You cried, and as I held back my own tears, I gently leaned my body in as much as I could to simulate a hug. Your memory was intact, and you definitely understood everything that was being said, so I began talking to you to try lifting your spirits. I told you that David had been there to see you, but that just made you ball even harder. And at that moment, your father walked in, surprised to see you awake...

"Hey, Cam!" The sound of your father's booming voice created a waterfall of tears that ran over your high cheek bones and visibly showed your mixed emotions. You were scared, confused, hurting and happy…all at the same time. I wiped your face and cleaned the building dried secretions with a damp cloth, assuring you that everything was going to be okay.

Your father configured the wireless speaker and found some appropriate music, while I hooked the portable fan to the bed rail and adjusted the temperature to a comfortable setting. I then began to rub your hands with the shea butter that filled the room with a fresh homey scent. You were so relaxed and finally at ease.

The neurologist ordered an MRI for you and scheduled it for the next day. Because you had also been in a car accident, the doctors wanted to check to see if you had any neck injuries. If not, they would remove the neck brace that you'd been wearing since the paramedics put it on you at the scene of the crime.

The medical team recommended that you now wear a helmet to protect your head because you were moving around so much. Because part of your skull had been removed, there was nothing in place to cover your brain other than soft tissue. You had a number of raw incisions, staples, and stitches all over the right side of your head, so this soft blue head gear was now part of your ongoing recovery process. Whenever you were out of the bed, you needed to wear it because you were a "Fall Risk." The nurses said that you were lucky to have been given such a fancy helmet, as most patients they'd seen with head injuries had to wear a hard, baseball helmet-like contraption.

The occupational therapist later came by to see you to begin working on your limbs. She introduced herself as Jessica and said that she'd schedule to see you a couple times a week while you were in ICU. She facilitated a physical orientation to determine what exactly you could and couldn't do and immediately felt a connection to you. She was confident that you would make a full recovery but was honest with her prediction of how much work and dedication it would require. She believed in you and was rooting for you.

Jessica gave us the following set of instructions:

- **Don't talk to the doctors about you in front of you—you can hear!** I just smiled. Jessica confirmed my uneasy feeling behind Dr. Hobbs' comments and justified my recent conversation with her. I already liked Jessica.
- **Come up with a system to communicate with you.** YES vs. NO. We'd decided on squeeze our hands once for YES, and squeeze our hands twice for NO.
- **Massage and move your feet and ankles frequently.** Again, I was already on the right track with the shea butter just earlier today. *Perfect.*

Your room was calm, peaceful, and a decent environment for healing…as best as possible, considering the circumstances. I mentally prepared myself to leave you for the night and began my ritual of prayer and oil distribution.

As I stepped out of your room, the head security guard rounded the corner to meet me at the Nurses' Station. He said he'd been looking for me and needed me to sign for your personal belongings. Turns out, during the attempted robbery, your assailants weren't able to get EVERYTHING from you, which is probably why they shot you.

We'd become quite friendly with the security team, all of

whom were men of different ages. They'd all heard your story and knew what had happened to you and took a personal interest in your recovery. The guard hesitated to hand the puffy manila envelope over to me, double-checking to be sure I was in the right state of mind to take it. After I thanked him and assured him that I was okay, he walked away to give me the privacy that he knew I needed.

I tore open the envelope and slowly pulled out the contents:

- two stretchy wrist bands that had been cut off your body by the medical staff;
- your gold rope chain, and still attached was a now blood-stained cross pendant;
- your Apple watch with your favorite white band, also splotched with dried blood;
- your red Frostburg State University cardholder, with your bank card, health insurance card, and driver's license still tucked in the slots;
- and five crisp $20 dollar bills, fresh from the ATM machine on your weekly payday…transaction receipt included.

I tucked all of these items back into the envelope and slowly put the package into one of my many bags. With so many questions in my head, I exhaled with the deepest sigh that I could stand. I somberly started my long walk through the hallways to leave you in the hospital. This was just still so hard to believe. *Lord, please cover my son…and me.*

# DAY 12

## DYING TO LIVE

One of the night nurses called bright and early, excited to tell me that you had remained stable throughout the night. She said that the order was submitted for your MRI, so you would be prepped early morning. I couldn't quite catch the name of the nurse on the other end of the phone, but most of them seemed to now look forward to being the designated person to contact me with a daily report.

Without even saying a word, you had won over the hearts of several of the ICU staff. They were all rooting for you and had begun to realize that they were watching a miracle in the making. As protocol and unwritten law, the staff wasn't supposed to refer to "God" as the source of your recovery while they were on the clock. But when many of them had heard and seen me praying, they would secretly tell me that they'd been doing the same for you. You were an inspiration to everyone around you, and you didn't even realize it. You gave us all a sense of hope and challenged us to lean on our faith.

As strong as I THOUGHT I was, I'd surprised myself with the unexplainable strength that I'd recently displayed. Many days, I wished that there were a handbook or manuscript to follow, page by page…but unfortunately, such a document does not exist. I just took it one day at a time, one hour at a time, one moment at a time…allowing my faith and spirit to lead the way.

When I arrived at the hospital, you weren't in your room. The technicians had taken you away for your MRI, so I sat in the waiting room until you returned. Once you were settled back in your quarters, Nurse Joseph confirmed that the plan for the day was to take you off the ventilator. The machine setting was changed to a mode that would transition you to totally breathe on your own, while the medical team monitored you closely. We were asked to stay in the waiting room until the process was complete and you were breathing rhythmically, comfortably…safely.

I was more restless than ever, and the hard chairs in the waiting room would not allow me to sit for longer than a few minutes at a time. The minutes actually felt like hours!

The air conditioning was on "extra high," so I made my way to the basement floor of the hospital to purchase a cup of hot chocolate from the outdated vending machine. When the warm taste of my favorite flavor failed to calm my nerves, I decided to take a walk to the gazebo that stood right outside the main entrance of the hospital. There, I was sure to find some peace and quiet so I could meditate and warm up a bit. But after about only ten minutes, I noticed a woman heading in my direction, talking out loud into the speaker of her cell phone.

The half-dressed, unnecessarily loud intruder sat on the bench directly across from me and never glanced my way to acknowledge my presence or say hello. Rolling my eyes, I shifted my body slightly to one side in frustration and let out a heavy sigh, hoping that she would get the message. If the stranger had looked up, I'm sure my non-poker face would've shown exactly how annoyed I was. Initially, I couldn't understand how Charlie Brown's school teacher kept finding me, and this time she was disguised as a hood rat. I waited for an appropriate break in her conversation to nicely ask her to lower her voice but that moment never presented itself.

But as I began to listen closely to her conversation for the most opportune time to speak, I was reminded that she was also a visitor at the hospital. Slowly, my heart connected with hers. I realized she was a mother, awaiting news about her son who had suffered multiple gunshot wounds. And immediately, I was ashamed of myself for being judgmental in the same way I'm sure that so many had been of me.

Though his story was different from yours, the current scene and aftermath was the same. The gazebo brought two women together to release some impatient, misplaced energy. She respected my process, and I now respected hers more. But unfortunately, her form of expression was a distraction for me. So, I quietly whispered a request to God to heal this stranger's son, who I'm sure looked a lot like my own, and then I began my walk back to the hospital entrance.

Three hours had passed before your nurse walked into the waiting room with good news. Your MRI results were good and did not show any nerve damage. Your breathing had also remained stable, so the medical team turned off the ventilator and removed the accompanying tubes from your mouth and throat.

We celebrated with smiles and praises and were very anxious to see you. *CAMERON!!!* You had started looking more and more like YOU, Son! You were wide awake and sitting up when we walked into the room, and you immediately grinned when you saw us. Right away, you tried to talk, but your words came out more like groans and growls because your throat was painfully scratchy and sore from being intubated for so long.

The one thing you said to us that we could clearly make out was "I LOVE YOU." The nurse laughed as she shared that you'd also said, "HEY," to get her attention earlier. You were struggling to verbally communicate, and knowing you, it wouldn't be long before you were telling jokes. Your eyes are mainly looked to the left, but we noticed how much you were trying to also shift them to the right. The nurse recommended that we stand on your right side which would give you a focal point and further help with this process.

A doctor soon came in for your routine assessment of any new progress or setbacks. He began to give you commands, and one could hear a pin drop in the room as we all stood extremely still and silent to watch.

You still could not move your left arm, which I knew was frustrating for you, considering that you're left-handed. You were able to lift your right leg a little higher than before, but the movement of your left leg was about the same. However, the toes on your left foot could wiggle like the little piggies in the nursery rhyme.

You were putting in work with your right extremity to extend strong hugs to all of us, squeezing our hands, giving thumbs up, and offering a closed fist "pound" to your father. You eventually became a little too comfortable with your movements, and the nurse was forced to tie your arm to the bed. You'd pulled out your IV and had tried to remove your neck brace on your own terms. *That's our Cameron!*

You had a really long, but amazing day. It was time to rest. *Thank you, Lord.* My plan was to continue to pray for a peaceful night and more great days ahead. I was watching a true miracle! God's so good!

*#CamStrong*

# DAY 13

## WHEN WE ARE STRONG, OUR STRENGTH WILL SPEAK FOR ITSELF

We were asked to be at the hospital as early as 10 a.m. so that we could meet with the neurologist to get a full download and understanding of your status. In looking closely at the results of your MRI, the doctor assured us that there was no additional bleeding or nerve damage in your head or neck. The only visible blood blockage was where the bullet had entered the right side of your brain and was later surgically removed.

The doctor expected that over time this obstruction would dissipate, and the wound would heal on its own. You will need to be reassessed continuously with routine MRIs and related tests to monitor progress or any potential setbacks. This was all positive news! And because of this, the doctor submitted an order to remove your neck brace. By late morning, it was taken off, and I could finally see your full face again, Son. You were slowly but surely looking more like yourself.

You continued to try to talk, but the after-effects of the ventilator were lasting. Your throat was still uncomfortably sore and scratchy, so you sounded like a character from the Marvel movie: *Avengers: Endgame*. When you attempted to talk, you tightly closed your eyes and your facial expression slightly turned into a frown. We encouraged you to rest your voice, but being the persistent rebel that you are, you continued through the pain. In the meantime, we could make out a handful of your growls:

- I love you.
- Yes.
- No.
- I'm not sleepy.
- Take this off.
- I want to go home.

You were actively squirming in the bed quite a bit…partly trying to get comfortable, and partly in pain. We all worked as a team to keep your pillows fluffed, adjust your layered blankets to accommodate the changing temperature, perfectly angle the portable fan, and keep your feet proportionately balanced. But no matter what we did, the strange uncomfortable hospital bed was still a strange uncomfortable hospital bed.

You were fidgety and anxious, still unsure of what had happened to you. And though you hadn't mentioned being hungry, it had been 13 days since you'd last eaten, and your body had started to show signs of malnourishment. Less body fat meant less cushioning for the firm mattress, and you were feeling every prick, turn, and tube. Unfortunately, you were barely able to swallow and definitely unable to eat. Therefore, the medical team deduced the need for a feeding tube, which was later administered through your nose.

The fluid that once filled your lung continued to break up, which resulted in massive amounts of mucus being produced in your nose and throat. Between your father and me, we worked the suction wand overtime to clear your passages, since you were unable to cough up this thick substance on your own.

The speech therapist Leslie visited with you later in the day to access not only your ability to speak, but also your ability to swallow. Who knew that SWALLOWING was such a process? And one that you had to now work on to do correctly. She introduced you to small pieces of ice chips to determine how your lips would move and whether or not the reflex of your tongue could manage swallowing. You carefully grabbed a piece of ice with your lips off her plastic spoon and slowly worked it around your mouth…then swallowed. The intensified sound of your gulp filled the quiet room as we all resembled mannequins, listening like *EF Hutton* was revealing a new stock tip. With cautious optimism, we all exhaled with relief when you smiled, signifying to Leslie that you wanted another ice chip. Her heart melted, and we all quietly celebrated just loud enough for you to hear the encouragement. "You're doing good, Cam!" The cold, tasteless mass felt good along the sides of your dry mouth, simulating a source of food and water. You continued to motion to Leslie, ice chip, after ice chip, after ice chip…until we could hear her scraping the bottom of the empty cup. Your speech therapist had become your new favorite person, ever…and you hers.

As your pain continued, Nurse Doris offered you several doses of Fentanyl throughout the day. It hurt me to see you in so much discomfort, and feeling helpless just drove the dagger in deeper. After several hours of waiting, the "official" results from your X-Ray were finally available and clearly determined that the temporary feeding tube had been properly threaded down to your stomach. The medical team could begin giving you nutrients directly, along with your regular doses of Oxycodone for pain.

As the sun set for the day, you were finally settling down. David came back into town and immediately made a beeline to the hospital from the highway. He visited with you for several hours into the night, just sitting at your bedside, talking to you, and playing your favorite music.

I returned to the waiting room to do some reading, giving you both some privacy and alone-time. You got teary-eyed and emotional from the mere mention of various people...and your brother was one of those people. I can only imagine how you expressed yourself to him, especially since you could only manage to grunt a few words. As much as it may have hurt for you to talk, I was sure you had a lot to tell him.

*We love you, Son...and we are right here with you fighting through this. Be strong, Cam!*

*#CamStrong*

# DAY 14

## DO BLACK LIVES REALLY MATTER?

On my early morning drive to the hospital, I was filled with an eerie, angry feeling. The sun looked and felt a little different than usual, and the streets seemed to be less busy with cars. It almost felt like I was on "auto-pilot," not even fully aware of the required stops, turns, and merges that I obviously had to make in order to reach my destination. Even after praying out loud for a second time already for the day, my spirit still felt uneasy.

I was thankful that my baby boy was pulling through an unimaginable injury. I was thankful that the night-shift nurse called this morning with an uneventful overnight report. I was even thankful that I was able to whip out the monthly parking pass to enter the hospital garage at a discounted rate. But I could not seem to shake this ungrateful feeling of rage, despair, and disappointment.

I was certain that the staff at the front desk would expect my same warm greeting when I picked up my visitor's badge. I was pretty sure that the Gift Shop and Cafeteria workers would anticipate my welcoming wave as I walked the long, spiraling halls and passed them with a bounce in my step. And I was confident that my son would need positive energy from me when I approached his bedside…not THIS stank side of me.

So, after I squeezed my car into a tight space and folded down my side mirrors, I lugged my bags out to the gazebo to sit for a while and gather myself. I allowed the cooler than normal sun to beam on my face while the approaching fall air traded with small pockets of humidity. I needed a minute.

There had been much recent buzz and demand for justice for another young Black man who was recently killed by law enforcement…this time in Austin, Texas. My social media platforms blew up with articles, pictures, videos, and expressive posts calling for boycotts and courses of action that are honestly useless at the end of the day. And sadly, there will be a next time…resulting in the same cycle.

My heart went out to each young Black and Brown person who had lost their lives at the hand of a privileged police officer or racist person, and I felt pain for the communities shaken up by this continuous injustice.

BUT, as I sat in front of the hospital, the calm was so much more disturbing. Where the hell was the angry mob of rioters for MY son? Where were the signs and the blowhorns? Why weren't people outraged that MY son, a young Black man, was shot in the head and left for dead by another Black man? Why do WE only get angry enough to try to make a difference when someone of another race, culture, or creed wrongs US? Is it possible that those outside of our bubble feel so comfortable to disrespect, hurt, and kill us because it's become so common for us to do it to ourselves?

My son's tragedy happened with no rhyme, reason, nor remorse. No one cared that he was fighting for his life, and his new norm would be nothing like it was just 2 weeks ago…and at the hands of someone who looks like him. There were no angry posts from popular social justice activists. No community manhunts. No calls to action. Just me, a mother on an emotional roller coaster, alone in a piss-infested gazebo, struggling for answers.

Something was definitely wrong with this picture. But because my son's case was "under investigation," I had to be quiet and contain the fire in my belly that was anxious for justice. Until then, my focal point would remain on the rehabilitation and medical advocacy for a miracle in the making that I was honored to watch. This too was of great importance. *But, Honey…just wait.* I picked up my bags and made my way to the front entrance of the hospital. With my daily painted-on smile, "Good morning…!"

You had no major changes throughout the day. The nurses simply tried to manage your pain and keep you comfortable. They worked to find a good regimen and combination for your pain medication. Your vitals remained stable, and you literally slept ALL DAY! Your grandparents came to the hospital to visit, but we all just spent the majority of our time in the waiting room, watching the news reports of protests, riots, and looting. Though there was much unrest throughout the country, I was grateful that a young Black man in Bed #5 was resting comfortably for the moment.

*Prayers continued! Be strong, Cameron! We love you!*

*#CamStrong*

# DAY 15

## BABY STEPS STILL MOVE YOU FORWARD

The night nurse told me that you had a good night, and the goal for the day was to simply manage your pain and to keep you comfortable.

David and I got to the hospital fairly early. Terri had been your assigned nurse for the day, with whom we were somewhat familiar. She told us that the medical team was planning to remove the staples from your head, which was a HUGE STEP! When the doctor arrived with very simple tools, I decided to step out of the room. As tough as my overall psyche had become, I still didn't think my stomach could handle watching several heavy-duty staples being pulled from my child's head with a set of jumbo tweezers. I'd just rather not take a chance of being lifted into a wheelchair again and waiting to regain consciousness. But your father stayed back to soak in the moment and later gave me the gory details. Another step towards allowing you to look more "normal." Progress!

Though pain management was the priority of the day, you suffered quite a bit. You grimaced by kicking your right leg off the side of the bed and allowing it to hang, which I supposed gave you some sort of comfort. Your feet and ankles were strapped in big blue space-like Velcro compression boots that were anchored with heavy plastic kickstands that helped to balance your legs. This footwear was necessary because you had been immobile for so long, and wearing them kept your feet and ankles straight. Without them, you probably would not have been able to walk again without either being pigeon-toed or slue-footed. So unfortunately, we had to put your leg back in place every time you hung it off the bed.

You were overwhelmingly restless and eventually pulled your feeding tube from your nose out of frustration. *CAMERON!* The medical team was inclined to administer a new set of tubing, which caused you even more discomfort. You could barely breathe because of the accumulated secretions in your nose and throat, and the suction wand did not work fast enough. Because you'd started biting on it, the suction lost some of its force. The respiratory therapist had to work on you a couple of times, and she tried to get you to cough up the lingering thick substance from your body. Thank goodness the fluid had moved from your lung! We just needed it to be completely removed from your body.

You were able to tell us that you were in pain and used your fingers to indicate the level of intensity. On a scale of 1-5, one finger meant you were having the least pain, and five fingers meant you were having the most. You held up a FIVE. Almost every hour, the nurse continued to give you Oxycodone through the feeding tube, with an accompanying dose of Fentanyl. You were able to sleep in spurts right after you were given all of those powerful medications, but you were clearly HIGH AS A KITE.

Watching you in such agony was just unbearable, but then seeing you look like a dope fiend enjoying his latest fix was even more troubling. I couldn't wait until you got past that point. *But in the meantime, stay strong, Baby. We are here with you every step of the way.*

In the midst of this real-life horror story, I received an unexpected call. The friendly voice on the other end of the phone was familiar...and timely. One of my colleagues with whom I'd grown close over the last few years was in the lobby of the hospital to offer me a hug and a shoulder. Cheryl's face was a sight for sore eyes as I turned the corner to approach the busy open area. I looked and felt a little disheveled but was sure that my smile temporarily shined through more than anything else. We sat and talked for a while, and my sister-coworker-friend's face was filled with concern as I gave her a complete run down of all that had happened with you. Cheryl offered her prayers and support, while handing over an envelope full of cash and two large bags of food, snacks, and random goodies on behalf of some of my colleagues. I was thankful, but speechless.

My college girlfriends later arrived at my house at approximately 6 p.m. and waited in their cars until I could get there. Because the goal for the remainder of the day was to keep you in a heavily sedated state so that you could rest, I'd agreed to come home a little early to take my girls up on the offer to clean my house from top to bottom.

They each knew how meticulous I could be about my home (borderline anal), but lately I hadn't been available either physically or mentally to keep up with my usual chores. My tribe showed up dressed in their best "Cleaning Lady" attire, stocked with Pine-Sol, Lysol, mops, gloves, dust feathers, and more! They'd also coordinated with my man-friend so that he could take me to the nail salon while they were working. I was sure that my feet and hands looked like that of a T-Rex from *Jurassic Park*. And although I hadn't really noticed or cared, I took the hint and appreciated the acts of kindness.

After a couple of hours receiving a relaxing manicure and pedicure, I returned home to my spotless castle that was filled with fresh lemon smells and loving smiles. My heart was so full from the outpouring of love from so many people. It was all such an incredible blessing. I appreciated every single gesture of care and support more than words could even begin to describe.

# DAY 16

## SOMETHING TO LOOK FORWARD TO

The night shift nurse called with a routine update first thing in the morning. You had rested through the night pretty well, and your vitals remained stable. This was good news, which made me feel a little more comfortable about my plan to leave the hospital before nightfall again. Stevie Wonder could see how exhausted I was these days, and one of my closest friends decided to help give me a little break. I reluctantly accepted her offer and almost felt guilty about not being at your bedside from sun-up to sundown. However, your father encouraged me to take a breather and assured me that he would keep me posted with any relevant information while I was away. So, as I made my daily early morning drive to the hospital, it actually felt good to have something to look forward to. Deep down, I secretly hoped that this did not make me a bad mother.

Throughout the day, you unfortunately suffered again with quite a bit of pain. You were starting to speak just above a whisper, able to now verbally communicate that you were hurting. Because you were no longer in a "critical condition" status, it felt as if your nurses spent a lot of their time tending to other patients. The idea was to give you pain medication to hold you over while they worked in other rooms and until you needed the next dosage. Your father, David, and I stayed in the room with you constantly so that you could tell us what you needed, and we in turn found your nurse Shariff to make requests on your behalf: "I'm in pain," "I'm hot," "I need to do #2." We had become the regular runners and assistant nurses for Bed #5.

You were having some flatulence that sounded more and more like an old car back-firing in a traffic jam! You somehow found this funny, which meant that your sense of humor had not been altered one bit. And the unpleasant smells caused each of us to momentarily scurry out of the room to catch our breath. You finally announced that you needed to have a bowel movement, which indicated that your body was trying to become more regular. Afterwards, your pain level dropped from a 5 to a mere 4, and you requested more pain medication. However, Shariff explained that he could only offer you a mild sedative at that time to help you relax, and you seemed to be satisfied with the alternative.

You had spent sixteen days in bed, around the clock...day in and day out. You had nothing but time on your hands to think, and I can only imagine what had been going through your mind. You'd become very emotional and sorrowful, and you cried frequently. We could barely understand what you said as you wept, but we assured you constantly that we were with you...and you were not alone.

I knew that this had been very difficult for you, and more than anything, I just wished that I could trade places with you to bear your burden. To take your mind off things, I softly massaged your hands with shea butter and helped you with some of the therapy techniques that Jessica showed us. You had started to slightly move your left hand and got a little feeling back. *Thank God...even for the baby steps and small successes!*

Later, your father encouraged you to do your breathing techniques that the respiratory therapist instructed, even when you didn't feel like it. It was very important that you did something every day in order to get better and continue progressing.

Once you were finally able to relax, I felt like it was a good time to slide out. I explained to you that Miss Belinda and her mom had given me a complimentary room at a fancy hotel for the night, and I was going to use it as an opportunity to relax a little myself. You gave me your stamp of approval by extending your right arm for a hug and telling me that you loved me. "I will see you tomorrow," you said with a grin, and I confirmed without a doubt. I reluctantly backed out of the room, slowly, as if I was a teenager sneaking out of her sleeping parents' room. And with that same feeling of guilt that crept into my spirit earlier that morning, my eyes welled up as I put my head down and swiftly walked away. I texted Tom to let him know that I was on the way.

Tom and I had attended high school together, and I hadn't seen him since Graduation Day in June 1989. Over the last few years, we'd connected virtually on social media and had only communicated with occasional friendly banter. It had only about two months before your incident that we exchanged phone numbers and decided to actually *talk*, and later meet for light fare and drinks. Our first outing turned into several more phone conversations and outings, which led to real interest in one another...potentially. On that dreadful afternoon, Tom was one of the few people I called to inform that you'd been shot, and he was in turn one of the first people who arrived to the hospital. Neither of us were probably thinking straight at the time. We both just acted in the moment. But over that next 24 hours, I didn't suspect that he would stick around, and I honestly didn't care. My only focus was your survival, and whether or not *I* could survive without *you*. Besides, my courtship with my old classmate was too fresh, and neither of us could have ever anticipated the curve ball that our brand-new love affair had been thrown. He hadn't asked for *this* when he'd invited me out on a series of dates.

What guy in his right mind could handle *this* drama, when I could barely wrap my own mind around it?

However, two weeks had elapsed since your shooting, and Tom was not only still calling, but he was my +1 for my evening getaway. He'd secretly arranged for balloons and champagne to be set up in the hotel room as a surprise for me, and went the extra mile to make sure that I smiled and relaxed, mentally and physically. As we settled in for the night, your father later called with an update as he left the hospital, reporting that you were resting nicely. *Thank God!*

Before I knew it, I found myself lying quietly and still just gazing through the opening of the curtains. The room was pitch black, only lit from the bright stars that shone through our window of the 18th floor. It must've been about 3 a.m., and I couldn't help but wonder what you were doing. *Were you asleep? Were you in pain?* All of a sudden, I once again felt like a criminal who had stolen valuable time from your bedside. I tried to muffle my cries so that I wouldn't wake Tom from his assumed slumber. But little did I know, he too had been lying awake thinking of you. Of *us*. He quickly reached for me and held me close while I openly cried…and trembled. I prayed aloud through deep breaths and gulps, and I sniffed after almost every other word. I begged God to show you mercy by replacing your pain with peace, allowing you to have a restful evening. Eventually, I cried myself to sleep, looking forward to laying my eyes on you again the next day.

*#CamStrong*

# DAY 17

## THE STRUGGLE IS REAL

Lori was assigned as your nurse last night, so she called me first thing in the morning to share her thoughts about you. She told me that your night was just "okay," unfortunately. You did manage to sleep some, but your pain level woke you up several times during the night and broke your rest. Though you were frustrated and fretful, there was careful decision-making around your pain medication dosages and the frequency of administration.

Because you were no longer on a ventilator, too many drugs in your system could result in your breathing becoming labored…or even stopping altogether.

Also, we've all heard the number of horror stories about prescription drug addictions that start from users being hospitalized. A patient can become so dependent on how much better a prescription drug makes them feel that the craving could begin to set in even when it isn't necessary at all.

And lastly, because of the type of injury that you'd sustained, unfortunately, you were going to have some pain sometimes. It was the job of the medical team to regulate it and keep you as comfortable as possible, finding a balance that wasn't harmful to you long-term.

I truly appreciated Lori's honesty and detailed explanation. I would never forget our frank and candid conversation. It gave me a greater understanding of this piece of the process and it better equipped me with the knowledge of being a good caregiver in the coming months.

Your father arrived at the hospital fairly early, allowing me to soak up every minute of the plush hotel room before check-out time. He encouraged me not to rush and assured me that everything was fine. But a mother's intuition is one that a father will never understand, and I knew better. However, I provided myself the time that I needed by giving your other parent more space in the pool of responsibility. I was thankful that your father had been at the hospital all but one day, but perhaps you could benefit even more from his presence by spending some time alone with him.

So, before I made my way to the hospital, I stopped to meet an old friend from high school to pick up the home-made meals that she'd lovingly prepared for our family. Tracy and I served on the Largo Alumni Committee, planning events that brought former classmates together through fundraising. We proudly made annual donations to our alma mater, and people genuinely looked forward to our functions. Our group had been on a hiatus for a couple of years, so it was not only good to see my former partner, but I was thankful to also receive this beautiful and timely gesture of support.

The love just kept pouring in for you, coming from all directions possible. After extending my many thanks and sincere hugs to my old friend, I headed to my next destination with the car smelling like baked chicken, salmon, cabbage, and rice. I couldn't wait to spread our dinner out on the back table of the ICU waiting room and dig in!

But once I arrived at the hospital, food was the last thing on my mind. I found that you had been struggling. Emotionally. You were feeling sorry for yourself and beginning to ask God that million-dollar question—"Why me?" You shed many tears, which I wiped away with a cool compress, rotating it to your forehead.

You don't realize just how strong you are until you are eye-level with your child who is confined to a bed and cannot do anything for himself—he cries while looking to you for answers. And you know that as his mother, you must fight back your own tears that are hidden in your heart, screaming to get out. So, you somehow manage to conjure up the perfect words of encouragement, without a single tremble in your voice or crack in your flow.

I spoke softly, "Cam, I'm here. Though we don't know *why* this happened, we *do* know that God spared you for a reason. You have a purpose in this life, and you're going to be just fine. You are strong, but it's okay to cry out sometimes. Lean on God. Ask Him for your continued strength and trust Him. And we're going to be with you every step of the way, and we'll all get through this together. I promise, Son."

You wouldn't look at me, but I could tell that you were listening to everything I said. And as you began to settle down, you coughed up quite a bit of the lingering secretions and allowed me to frequently use the suction wand to get it out. From that moment, you seemed to become more inspired as the day passed.

But me? Every thread of my soul was challenged and suffered from exhaustion, despite the overnight stay in a relaxing spa-like hotel room. And like during many other random moments over the last three weeks, I calmly walked into my favorite stall of the ladies' room and released the tears that had been clawing their way to the top of my ducts...and I screamed to the top of my lungs. No one rushed to my rescue or even came into the bathroom to inquire. I'm sure that my screams were an all too familiar sound that had leaked from this common hiding place of the Trauma Center before. I just happened to be the current occupant that day.

Your occupational therapist later came by to work with you. Jessica was tough, and she pushed you to the potential that she saw in you. Though you were down, she knew you weren't out...and she was committed to seeing you advance in your recovery while on her watch. She showed us how to move your head around to help exercise your neck muscles and also regain your strength and ability to balance.

I noticed that you'd been trying to lift your head at times, but with much difficulty. Somehow Jessica knew that her instruction was not only helpful, but also timely. Your head had been leaning to the right side ever since your neck brace was removed, but Jessica reiterated that you should be holding your head straight in the middle. This simple task would take some work, but it was important that you tried to correct your stance each time we noticed an inappropriate shift. Jessica also worked on your left arm and tried to get you to raise your shoulder, but you were not quite ready for the task just yet.

Jessica pulled out a contraption that looked like a miniature harp, but the strings were actually rubber bands. She assembled your fingers into the aligned holes and asked you to squeeze. The placement of the bands created the level of intensity, which was currently on the lowest setting. Your face cringed while you applied all your might, and we all watched you slightly move your left fingers several times as they struggled to grip the harp. I wiped the sweat from your brow and then replaced the washcloth with a proud kiss. I guess that motivated you to show off for Jessica even more, because you then softly squeezed her hand with your left fingers when she asked you to…something that you had yet to do for any of the doctors who had come by for their daily assessments.

This was a BIG DEAL, and we quietly celebrated the progress with you.

But Jessica didn't stop there—she wanted to push you to your limit and test your full potential. She showed us how to do some leg exercises with you, bending both of your long limbs at the knees and stretching out your calves. Though we were lifting your legs, we could feel you helping and applying your own force. This full body work-out wore you out completely, and your pain was at a Level 4. Nurse Kathy mixed up a cocktail of pain medication, and your father and I stepped out for a while so that you could rest.

*We are so very proud of you, Cam!*

Later that evening, Kathy dragged a huge chair around to your room and wanted you to sit in it. It looked like an outdated leather chair that Granddaddy used to have in the "Rec Room" years ago. I think we all gave her the side-eye, but if looks could kill, yours would've retired poor Kathy's nursing career right there on the spot! She definitely took your scowl as a hint, but she explained to us how the simple act of sitting could strengthen your muscles and doing so was part of your recovery. Without any argument or discussion, she left the clunky piece of furniture outside your room and made you reluctantly promise to try the next day.

*This should be interesting*, I thought.

Oddly, you'd started holding on to the secretions and

excess saliva, resistant to opening your mouth and making it impossible for us to suck it out. Your mouth was at its full capacity, and your face looked like it was going to explode! You were tired of the suction wand being poked around in your mouth, even though this process helped clear the stubborn remaining fluid from your body. The hose was already distorted because you'd bitten on it so much as a way to rebel, but now you wouldn't even let me get it past your teeth. Honestly, the whole thing was pretty disgusting. But you wouldn't believe the things I'd seen in the hospital during our stay, and I could only imagine what I would be exposed to in the near future.

Because your pain level had not subsided any, the doctors decided to increase your Oxycodone dosage from 10mg to 15mg, just to keep you comfortable. I totally understood the risks of addiction and altered breathing patterns, but my child was suffering. You hadn't had any solid rest in a few days now, so I was adamant about having your medications adjusted accordingly.

One thing I'd learned in this short journey thus far was that patient advocacy is key. You were definitely not in the right state of mind to make sound decisions or even to know what to ask for. Therefore, I was determined to do it for you.

FINALLY. You were asleep and resting comfortably.

*We are so proud of you, Cam! You had an amazing day! Keep up the good work, Son!*

*#CamStrong*

# DAY 18

## DELIRIOUS!

It was 7:00 a.m., and I wondered why Lori hadn't called me yet with your nightly report. Oh Lord, that could only mean ONE thing...something was wrong! Did you have some sort of relapse? Was your pain level so high that your blood pressure sky-rocketed again? Was your lung still filled with fluid because you're having a hard time getting up the stubborn phlegm? Did you pull out your IV because you were frustrated? Did you have too many pain medications in your system, and as warned, your body had an unthinkable reaction? *Oh Lord!*

I immediately went into prayer, asking God to cover you. "Father God, thank you for another day. Thank you for waking me up this morning and giving me another opportunity to love on my sons. Lord God, I pray that Cameron is safe and that he had a restful night, with comfort and peace...no pain. Lord I ask that you continue to give the doctors and nurses the knowledge and wherewithal to tend to my boy, giving him compassion and the best care humanly possible. I pray for a positive report, dear Lord, and that my son is still protected by the blood of Jesus. These blessings I ask in your name, Jesus Christ, my Lord. Amen."

With unsteady hands, I picked up my cell phone to scroll through my recent calls. I hit the most frequently called number listed, the direct landline immediately outside your room. I could barely breathe as I hit the speakerphone button and sat straight up in the bed.

Lori answered, and I could hear a frantic tone in her voice. My heart dropped. She hurriedly told me that she couldn't talk much now but explained to me why she hadn't called yet. You'd just had a huge bowel movement, and she was in the middle of cleaning you up.

"AHHHHHHHH!," I hollered in relief! I'd let my mind run wild with horrific thoughts, instead of relying on my faith.

Lauren called me back within 30 minutes and told me that you had a decent night. She had sat with you quite a bit just talking to you during her shift, and she even played some tracks from the J. Cole album to help keep you relaxed. She'd figured it out. Lori had self-diagnosed you with a classic case of loneliness, and she knew enough and cared enough to administer the perfect remedy.

When I arrived at the hospital, you were holding the purple stress ball that I gave you the night before. It was one of many random giveaways that I'd snagged at a meeting while on travel for work. Over the years, I'd attended countless events where I'd stuffed as many useless souvenirs in my registration bag as possible. Because you were trying to strengthen your hands while bed-ridden, a once meaningless token suddenly became a rehabilitation resource at a pivotal time.

However, the increase in pain medication had you in a dazed state, and though you were holding the stress ball, your hand wasn't moving at all.

YOU weren't moving. You weren't responding.

This was nothing like the day before, and it was actually a little scary. But I guess it's the trade-off to keep you comfortable and allow you to rest. The day nurse,

Vincent, would need to make some adjustments in spacing your doses of medication out a little more because I don't think this is what any of us want to see.

The doctors put in an order for a new medication that would help break up the pesky secretions that continued to linger in your throat and nose. It came in the form of a patch that was placed behind your left ear. It reminded me of the Dramamine patches that travelers wear for motion sickness when boarding a cruise ship. I kept my fingers crossed that this worked for you. Though you'd been coughing up a lot of thick mucus, and we'd been constantly sucking it out, it was just not enough.

You stayed in a deep sleep for quite some time, but that did not stop the respiratory therapist from coming in to routinely beat on your chest and back with her trusty suction cup. Penelope flipped you from side to side like a sack of potatoes, with no assistance from anyone...not even you. You were unbothered, and all of your vitals remained intact while she worked. You simply went right back to sleep after she completed her full process, just as she were never there.

*Wow. Unbelievable.*

When you finally woke up on your own, Vincent routinely checked all of your vitals again. Your blood sugar was at 101, and your temperature sat at 99. Both good.

You took a deep breath through your mouth and seemed to either be well-rested, in a good mood...or plain delirious! Suddenly, you came out of your comatose state and began smiling from ear to ear, literally laughing as you looked directly into each of our faces for the first time in weeks.

Did you think you'd just woken up from a bad dream? Or were you actually still asleep and dreaming with your eyes open? *Who knew, and who cared?!*

It was great to see your smile and hear a version of your laughter, nonetheless. For that moment, you really looked like yourself and I had MY SON back. You were still so incredibly handsome.

While in this happy state, your father easily convinced you to try your breathing treatment. You thought that blowing air into the plastic tubes was hilarious, and you continued to giggle after each puff! I massaged your hands with shea butter and then moved to your feet. You laughed uncontrollably, wiggling your toes to encourage me to keep going. To this day, I don't know if the motion of my fingers created a tickling sensation to you, or if you were just plain tickled. Either way, the memory is a priceless one.

Later in the day, you started to cough up some major amounts of phlegm and secretions, which seemed to wear you out...but made you feel a lot better. The "motion sickness" patch worked like a charm! Thank goodness. You felt well enough to start trying to talk again, although your voice was still raspy. And having the hiccups three times in one day didn't help. You were quite annoyed because there was nothing anyone could do to help you get rid of them, not even offer you a cup of water. Each time, you just had to wait for them to go away on their own.

Your cousin Rasheed was in town for a few days visiting from California. He stayed at Nana and Granddaddy's house the night before and rode with them to the hospital that evening to see you. This was actually the first time you'd been wide awake and 100% conscious during your grandparents' visit, so this would be a very different encounter.

As soon as they stepped into the room and Nana let out her grandmotherly, "Hiiiiiiii, Cam!," you burst into tears.

Unfortunately, she did not have as much control over her emotions as I'd grown to have, so she also cried as the two of you embraced. With happiness, sadness, and a host of other emotions, even your grandfather had to turn his back to shield his leaking eyes.

After several minutes of sniffling, snotting, and eye wiping, you finally turned to Granddaddy with a smile and noticed his newly grown, silver goatee.

"You look like Sheldon."

At first, your grandfather couldn't make out what you were saying, so you repeated it at least three times as he moved in closer with each attempt. Finally, you both shared an excited chuckle when he realized that you were referencing your favorite character on a popular television sitcom that you both watched and enjoyed.

This showed Granddaddy that you completely recognized him and that your memory was definitely intact...at least to the extent of your common interests. This meant the world to your grandfather, which made him even more emotional.

Rasheed sat in the waiting room for a while. Technically, we snuck him in because he was not on your official list for visitation. But luckily, Granddaddy has strong genes that stretch across generations, so the security guards thought Rasheed was David, and he breezed right through all the security protocol that had been put in place for your visitation.

When I asked you if it was okay for Rasheed to come in and see you, your eyebrows immediately lifted in surprise.

"RASHEED...MY COUSIN...RASHEED???," you asked in a raised whisper. When I confirmed, you just began to cry even more...uncontrollably. You actually became overwhelmed, and we decided that it might be time to end your visitation for the day and allow you to rest. Rasheed totally understood and agreed to try again the next day, as *this* day had been emotionally draining for you.

Vincent prepared another batch of Oxycodone, while your father played more of your J. Cole favorites on a low volume setting. Before long, you were sound asleep. It was a good day.

# DAY 19

## BE SOMEONE'S REASON TO NEVER GIVE UP

Your night nurse Erica called this morning with very little to report. She simply said that you had no problems through the night, your vitals remained stable, and you rested well. As usual, I appreciated the call and the update. Little news is good news these days.

When I arrived at your room, Vincent was preparing to put you in the special chair. "Hi, Ma," you murmured with no excitement at all. You were wearing the soft blue helmet on your head and looked totally uninterested in what was about to happen. You hated wearing this head gear, but because part of your skull was missing, nothing would protect your brain should you fall...and you were definitely considered a FALL RISK, according to the yellow band on your arm.

You are 6-feet tall, and Vincent quickly acknowledged that he was unable to handle your long, lanky body on his own. We waited for 20 minutes before two ladies from the nursing staff could tear away from their patients to assist with moving you from the bed to the chair. It was almost comical to watch them struggle with you because you were unable to help them at all with what seemed like a science fair project. You'd been confined to the bed for so long, the hospital staff must not have realized just how tall you actually were. The three nurses wrestled with your body, each giving their own set of instructions while shifting you around, trying to get you from one side of the room to the other. You towered over everybody but had no control over any of your limp limbs and felt almost embarrassed to be part of such a vulnerable scene.

FINALLY. You were slumped over in the chair and immediately appeared to be very uncomfortable. However, Vincent and his back-up team felt accomplished as they all exhaled, wiped their sweaty brows, and smiled after transferring all of your weight from their shoulders to the arms of the clunky chair.

Before returning to their posts, one of the nurses thought to pull out the leg rest on the front of the chair because your over-extended legs and protruding knees clearly looked awkward. The look on your face said it all. You wiggled your toes to indicate that you were still uncomfortable, and you said to me in a very irritable whisper, "I want to lay down."

Though you already knew, I reiterated that sitting in the chair was part of your recovery process and that you must do for a little while each day. We continued to encourage you for another 15 minutes, when Vincent returned to your room with a large pillow-like cushion. With a sheepish look, he admitted that he'd forgotten to put the padding in the chair first, which had probably added to your torture. We all agreed that it made sense to move you back to the bed for now, and we could try again the next day after making sure the chair was set up properly. We waited for all three nurses to reassemble and watched the cumbersome return to your bed.

After being still for a while and recovering from the unwanted action, we allowed your cousin to return for a visit. You were much calmer than you had been the day before, and it seemed like a good time, especially since he was traveling back to the West Coast tomorrow.

I escorted Rasheed to your doorway and announced that he was coming in. Though you cried a little, you were happy to see him and welcomed his company. Rasheed was your and David's one and only first cousin, and he had set the trendsetting standard for the young men of our family. Losing his mother at age 6 to breast cancer, my nephew beat all the stereotypical odds of an Black male growing up with a lot of uncertainty and mixed feelings about life itself.

Rasheed was nothing short of a self-made genius, and you and your brother looked up to him and valued his opinion on almost everything. I had no doubt that you were concerned about what your cousin would think when he saw you lying helplessly in your hospital bed; and as always, you'd hang on his every word, even in that moment. I stepped on the other side of the glass door and pulled it closed, giving the two of you some privacy. An hour later, Rasheed was gone, and you were in a better mood.

Your speech therapist then paid you a visit later in the day. Leslie was definitely your favorite person at the hospital! She was so upbeat and genuinely seemed to look forward to seeing and working with you. I think she was fascinated with your progress, and her excitement appeared to motivate you. Leslie announced that she had the *good* ice chips, but she was also carrying apple sauce in her bag. YUMMY! Though you had no expression on your face, your eyes darted in her direction at the mention of some type of food! You were able to grab small portions of the apple sauce from Leslie's plastic spoon and successfully swallow it. You then crunched on her pieces of ice like they were the last remaining potato chips in the bottom of the bag. You were happy. You talked a little bit, telling Leslie that you knew that August was the current month, but you weren't quite sure of the day of the week. When she asked if you knew your brother's name, with a wide smile, you whispered, "David." That moment warmed everyone's heart in the room, including Leslie's.

You slept for a few hours after getting your next dose of pain medication, but I was still very much concerned about how lethargic 15mg of Oxycodone left you. You were clearly DOPED UP and had begun to hallucinate. You'd seen unreal images of some of your favorite hip-hop artists, mistaking your own brother for a rapper named G-Herbo. You were excited to inform us that Jay Critch and Gunna were scheduled to visit the sick patients of the hospital in the coming days. And you swore to me that you'd seen Vincent somewhere before. From what I could make out of your growling whispers, he was in the operating room when you first arrived at the hospital, and you saw him take your Apple watch. At least these are the stories that the Oxycodone had you tell.

I spoke directly with the attending physician, Dr. Montego, about my concerns, and he agreed to decrease your next dosage to 10mg so that you could function again. He would gauge your pain level afterwards and take it from there. The doctor also expressed concerns about how you were not properly managing and swallowing your saliva. I explained to him that you were complaining that your throat and chest still hurt and that it was simply uncomfortable to swallow. You were also struggling to breathe through your nose because of the mucus build up. Dr. Montego listened to my updates and agreed to closely monitor you for the next 24 hours to rule out an infection. If a problem did not exist, he was going to put in an order to have your temporary feeding tube removed and surgically place one directly into your stomach. *Jesus…Another surgery.*

# DAY 20

## THE PAIN YOU FEEL TODAY WILL BE THE STRENGTH YOU FEEL TOMORROW

As soon as I arrived at the hospital, your case manager waved me down before I could reach your room. I had certainly appreciated her routine check-ins with me to inquire about our administrative needs and offer professional recommendations. We'd met Theresa Monroe on the first day that we arrived at the hospital. She was very pleasant and showed much compassion during a time I could barely hold up my head to talk to her. She explained that she would keep up with all of your needs and serve as a liaison for information regarding medical insurance, discharge, and any special administrative requests. In addition, her soft voice and caring aura always felt trusting and comforting when I consulted with her.

As usual, Ms. Monroe had been following your daily progress reports and advised me that it was time to begin researching rehabilitation hospitals. She explained that you would most likely need inpatient long-term acute care, which I had absolutely no idea what exactly that meant. She also warned me that most health insurance companies only fully cover 30 days of the related expenses. It was imperative that I contact my provider to verify our medical plan and coverage as soon as possible.

*Deep sigh.* I thanked Ms. Monroe for the information and anxiously continued to walk toward your room without giving what she'd told me much thought. The closer I got to your doorway, I did, however, remember that my health insurance coverage had proven to be nothing short of extraordinary, surprising many healthcare practitioners whenever I handed them my credentials to look up the details. I was positive that you'd get whatever medical attention you needed in this process but did not want to make any assumptions.

*NOTE TO SELF: Research "inpatient long-term acute care," and call the insurance company.*

Unfortunately, you'd been complaining about pain all morning. Dr. Montego worked with us to decrease your Oxycodone the night before...but sadly, you were not ready, and the medical team was forced to increase your dosage again. If 15mg was too much, and 10mg was not enough...why couldn't we try 12.5mg? *Seemed like common sense to fall somewhere in between, right?* I suggested this to the doctor, and he said he would consider it.

Your feeding tube was now clogged and wouldn't allow any nutrients to get down into your stomach. This was obviously a big problem because you were unable to eat on your own at all. According to the weight of the bed and your updated charts, you'd already lost approximately 30lbs over the last three weeks, and the expectation was that you would continue to wither away without your pre-injury food intake.

Unfortunately, the medical team had to put you through the very uncomfortable process of removing the malfunctioning tube and replacing it with a new one. We sat in the waiting room for a while so that the staff could work on you without any distractions. However, I couldn't sit still for long, so I decided to walk the hallways to find a quiet place to meditate and pray.

Once we returned to your room, I noticed that you were

having quite a bit of bleeding from your nose and mouth after the placement of the new feeding tube. Your assigned nurse Brandi explained that a little blood is normal, but she hurriedly grabbed a few cleaning supplies to tidy you up after feeling the rays of my wrath in her immediate space.

After you rested a while, Leslie cheerfully entered the room. Perfect timing! Her visits always seemed to cheer you up a bit. She fed you the usual ice chips, which were your favorite. But she also had a thick apple juice that almost looked like syrup. You used your lips to grab the unfamiliar substance from her plastic spoon, but upon trying to swallow it, you began to gag. You immediately began to cough, and reflex-tears filled your eyes. Leslie calmly noted that the syrup went down "the wrong tube" and used this as a teaching moment to explain to us the difference between the trachea and the esophagus. They are located very close to each other but completely differ in function. The trachea is the airway which allows us to breathe clearly, whereas the esophagus is the food pipe, where all substances should travel when we swallow. In your case, the syrup just went down your airway instead of your food pipe, causing you to cough and have trouble breathing. Science is so simple, but complicated at the same time. Ironically, after your coughing spell, your talking voice suddenly became stronger. Leslie sure had a way of bringing out the best in you.

The hospital's rehabilitation director, Kayla Green, stepped in the room to introduce herself during your speech therapy session. She excused herself, but Leslie was more than happy for her to join us. Ms. Green was a soft-spoken, middle-aged Black woman who reminded me of one of my aunts. She exuded compassion and a genuine care for you. Your story had traveled the halls of the hospital like rapid wildfire, and people were honored to meet and talk to you, from the cleaning staff to the hospital's head honchos with fancy titles. As always, you were respectful and pleasant as you answered Ms. Green's questions, and before long, she too fell in love with you. She knew that "the chair" had been brought into your room the day before and had heard about the mishap during your first attempt to sit in it. She asked if you'd do her a favor by trying to sit in it again while she was there and assured you that the padding had been appropriately installed to provide a better experience. Leslie cheered you on and even offered to help move you to the chair as a way to further encourage you. You trusted her. So, if she was on board, surely it was okay to give the chair another try.

Once you agreed, I carefully slid the much-hated helmet down your head and attached the Velcro straps around your chin. Your father chipped in as a third reinforcement, assisting the ladies in transporting you out of the bed, across the floor, and safely into the chair. This was a much better transition than what I had witnessed with Vincent and his goons the other day. Ms. Green and Leslie propped you up as much as possible with a pillow and covered your bare legs with a blanket to keep you warm. I didn't know if you were more uncomfortable from the chair or from the vulnerability you felt in the presence of the two women who crowded around you with unbelievable care. Your face was long and sad, and your body slumped over because you were unable to control your muscles in sitting up. Ms. Green kneeled down so that she became eye-level with you and explained that what you were feeling was normal. As tears began to ravish your face, she continued to talk to you. She promised you that you were going to be fine, telling you that it was okay to cry, but that you should never give up. Ms. Green reminded you of how strong you were, and that your youth and athleticism were going to play an important role in your rehabilitation. It was going to be hard, and it would be a lot of work...but she believed in you and was confident that you were going to make it. As you cried, I had to turn away and step out of the room to shed my own tears.

As the night began to fall, you started to complain about some discomfort in your neck. This was new. We initially thought it was from the weird position you had been lying in for hours after having the new feeding tube put in your nose. But in reality, the car crash could have resulted in whiplash or some other type of injury. You also had an unexplained contusion on the top of your forehead, and the speculation was that you probably had hit your head on the steering wheel of the car upon impact. No one will ever know what really happened in the crash other than you. And unfortunately, you didn't remember any of it. Before Brandi ended her shift, she brought in a heating pad to place on the side of your aching neck, and this gave you some temporary relief.

The ICU unit had settled down for the night, and I was beat. Strangely, you were still wide awake and appeared to want continued company. Your father assured me that it was okay for me to go home to get some rest, and he would stay with you as long as necessary. You needed your dad, now more than ever. And I felt comfortable enough to leave you in his hands tonight.

A few hours later, Gary's number flashed on my cell phone, and I immediately picked up. I think I subconsciously anticipated his call, so I was hesitant to fall asleep, despite how tired my body felt. He'd just left the hospital and was heading home for the night, but he wanted to tell me about his late-night visit with you. Leslie had okayed us to feed you ice chips whenever you wanted them, so your father had a cup-full handy. This simple treat seemed to relax you and give you temporary satisfaction. The two of you listened to trap music but turned the volume down low enough so as not to disturb other patients. In the dark room illuminated only by the main lighting from the common area, you talked…a lot. You asked questions about why you were in the hospital because you still didn't really know, and it was at that time that you shared your assumption of having been in a car accident. You couldn't remember any details, but it seemed like the most sensible solution. Your father confirmed your curiosity to help settle your mind and told you where you were at the time of the crash. When he asked you if you remembered anything else, he could almost see your mind working, full of jumbled thoughts, trying to recollect something…ANYTHING. You made no mention of being shot, and you had no idea who you were with, where you were, or why you were there. You couldn't even remember much about the day or hours leading up to the event. Your father told me that you were very calm, and the two of you had a great conversation. When he left you, you'd fallen asleep in decent spirits, content with knowing that you had survived a mere car accident. Now, it was up to us to figure out how to tell you that there was so much more to your story.

One funny thing that your father mentioned before we ended our call was that your "condom" catheter came off and you peed in the bed. Your night nurse Bill was not happy about having to clean you up and change your bed during the midnight hour. Remember when he lied and didn't tell me that you'd had a difficult night during one of his prior shifts? *Welp…Karma is a bitch, Billy Boy.*

## DAY 21

# FROM THE ROOTER TO THE TOOTER

Whenever Bill was your night nurse, I didn't expect a call in the morning. I was prepared to call him, as usual. When I did finally get him on the phone to ask him about an overnight report, I chuckled to myself from the mere thought of his face while cleaning up your pee. However, I appreciated Bill for simply doing his job, and I've grown to understand that not everyone will go above and beyond their standard duties. He told me that you had complained about pain a couple times during the night, but he was able to manage it by giving you medication as needed. Your vitals had remained stable, and you had been cleared for your surgical procedure today.

One of the first things that I did when coming into your room after saying hello and kissing your cheek was to check your white board for the noted daily goals and expectations. I noticed that you were assigned two day nurses for the day, Tina and Zoe. Initially, I was surprised and excited to think that you would be continuously monitored with two nurses rotating your coverage. But I quickly realized throughout the day that your immediate attention remained very limited. Go figure.

Although you had complained about pain in your head, your nose, your neck, your collar bone, and about just being in the BED overall, you still managed to be somewhat upbeat. You were excited about having the temporary feeding tube taken out of your nose and having the permanent one surgically placed in your stomach. You were extremely talkative, allowing your sense of humor and personality to shine through. With almost a straight face, you told us that the nurses are "running around like chickens with their heads cut off!" It was so refreshing to hear you not only talk but also crack jokes and chuckle. Exactly how long had you been lying here, playing possum, watching everybody, and paying attention to everything? I was sure you had a funny story for every person who'd dared to venture into the room of Bed #5. *THAT'S my boy!*

The surgeon who would install your feeding tube came by to see you first thing in the morning. Dr. Roberts put a straw down in a cup of water and asked you to sip. He wanted to confirm whether or not you could swallow, and once he saw that you could, he allowed you to sip away! You had been complaining about thirst, so you were happy to gulp down as much water as possible; afterwards, letting out a loud belch. However, your speech therapist soon received word that you'd taken advantage of an opportunity to drink, and she was not happy. News travels fast! Leslie immediately came by your room to confirm the grapevine and was on a mission to find Dr. Roberts to scold him. She explained that water could cause exasperation because it could mistakably and easily go down your airway, instead of your esophagus, causing pneumonia of the lungs...and we definitely did not want that again. OOPS! We didn't know the risks, and apparently neither did Dr. Roberts. But we would definitely be more aware going forward if put in the situation again. Thank goodness you were okay, and there were no mishaps. But since you'd had a taste of the sweet life, you were begging EVERYBODY that came into your room for water! Doctors, nurses, technicians, WHOEVER. You even asked your father and me to smuggle water into your room, but I refused to be on Leslie's bad side.

Your surgery was scheduled for 1:00 p.m., but after a couple of hours passed, we were told that the operating room was backed up from other surgeries. We patiently waited while you napped on and off, listening to music, and Dr. Roberts finally came in around 4:30 p.m. to announce that he was ready to get started with your procedure. The look of relief on your face was priceless, as we watched the technicians fold up the arms of your bed and roll you out of the room. After blowing kisses to you, I shed a single tear and immediately went into prayer. I could finally stop ignoring the loud grumbles that came from my stomach and exhale long enough to visit the crowded cafeteria on the ground level of the hospital.

When stressed, some people can barely eat and shed several pounds as a result of starving themselves or simply forgetting to eat. But me? I'm the exact opposite! As a bonified stress-eater, I'd been stuffing whatever food I could find in my mouth over the last few weeks. It's helped that our supportive friends and family delivered home-cooked dishes and full-blown meals to the hospital or to wherever I lay my head on a particular evening. I always woke up to food…and it was very much welcomed! I attacked the half-stocked vending machines every chance I got, just to exert some misplaced energy whenever I needed to take a short walk. Over the year leading up to your shooting, I'd worked hard to maintain a sexy weight and physique as I re-entered the dating scene. But now, with my tray piled up with two pieces of fried chicken, mashed potatoes with gravy, green beans, a slice of apple pie for dessert, and a Diet Pepsi, I could definitely feel that my favorite pair of leggings were starting to fit differently. *Bon Appetit!*

The doctor told us that the surgery was a success, and he did not run into any problems during your procedure.

The temporary feeding tube had been removed from your nose, and a different tube was now protruding from your stomach that would be used to give you needed nutrients. You were still talking a lot, but this time expressing how much discomfort you were in and begging for medication. But little did you know, your scheduled dosage had already been administered, so we hoped that it would kick in momentarily to relieve you of the pain.

Interestingly enough, you soon began telling us again that Vincent stole your watch while he was cleaning you up in the operating room. You were very detailed and descriptive with this particular story, and for a quick second, we were starting to believe you! Did you really remember Vincent…or someone who resembled him in the operating room? Maybe you recalled someone quickly stripping off your clothes and jewelry so that the doctors and medical team could initially work on you in the Emergency Room? The medical report DID state that you were awake and talking upon arrival, so God only knows what you thought you saw or remembered. All I know is that you were convinced that this man had your watch. But unbeknownst to you, the non-functioning watch was included in the bag of your personal belongings that the security guard handed to me weeks ago. The hallucinations were somewhat troubling but a little comical at the same time. We let you talk and exist in your own little world for the time being, finding our own solace in knowing that this too would pass.

One of your two nurses came in for a routine check and noted that all your vitals were normal, and everything looked good. When Tina mentioned that she would return shortly to re-dress your bed sores, suddenly and without warning, Charlie Brown's school teacher magically appeared again.

*Wait. WHAT?! BED SORES??? How? When? Where?!*

This was a TOTAL surprise to us, and we were caught completely off guard. Not ONE nurse had mentioned anything to us about you having bed sores, until NOW...and we definitely wanted some immediate information. Your nurse explained that there were two lesions on your buttocks, which were documented in your chart as Stage 2 bed sores. "Are you serious?!," I rhetorically asked.

There are generally four stages to this condition:

- ***Stage 1:*** The area looks red and feels warm to the touch;
- ***Stage 2:*** The area looks more damaged and may have an open sore, scrape, or blister;
- ***Stage 3:*** The area has a crater-like appearance due to damage below the skin's surface;
- ***Stage 4:*** The area is severely damaged, and a large wound is present.

So, this meant that someone either missed the Stage 1 diagnosis, or just failed to reveal this information to us. UNACCEPTABLE! I didn't want to be rude or fuss at poor Tina because she just happened to be your nurse today. And frankly, she was the one who gave us this new information, even if it was by accident. She actually thought we already knew. She was at a loss for words and did not have many answers beyond what she had already told us. But Tina did reiterate the purpose of the cushioned wedges that were used to supposedly turn you from side to side every hour. They prevented you from lying on your backside, or any side, for long periods of time, decreasing the chance of developing bed sores. This obviously meant that you hadn't been moved around in the bed enough, considering that your condition had reached its second stage. I supposed this was the down-side of being upgraded from "critical condition" to a mere "serious condition."

Both your father and I were irate, and we realized that Tina was remorseful and overwhelmed. I told her that we wanted to speak with the charge nurse, who supervised all the staff responsible for this task. Within minutes, we were escorted through what felt like a secret trap door and down a maze-like hallway, finally reaching the ICU administration office and sitting down in front of the person whom we wanted to see.

Teddy was a tall, dark-complexioned man with an accent that sounded of African descent. He'd already been briefed on why we were there, and he knew your story from start to finish like most of the hospital staff. With much concern in his voice, before we could even start with our boiling rant, he began with an apology and immediately accepted accountability for the situation on behalf of his staff.

"There's no excuse. But I can assure you that I will personally tend to your son's wounds and make sure his condition is continuously monitored every hour," Teddy said with confidence. It quickly felt as if this was a complaint that Teddy had heard from family members like us before, and he was prepared and more than willing to spring into action to put our minds at ease. "I will examine him right now to get a better sense of the needed treatment."

Teddy stood up from the chair behind his desk and invited us to follow him back through the staff route of the ICU pods, returning to your room. The intense LED lights over your bed seemed to be turned up to 1,000, and your room was the brightest I'd ever seen it. Teddy meant business! He introduced himself to you with a smile and told you that he'd heard a lot about you. His voice was calming and reassuring. He called both of your day nurses into the room for assistance and belted out detailed instructions to them as he reached for two blue plastic gloves, snapping them snuggly onto his hands and fingers. Tina and Zoe followed the direct orders and carefully positioned you for a supervisorial visual assessment. And sure enough, peeking over the shoulder of Teddy's white coat, I could see the lesions on your body that had caused this impromptu commotion. Teddy loaded two of his fingers with the medicated ointment that was a sure remedy for this type of wound and confidently applied it, as necessary. He spoke out loud for us all to hear, "This young man needs to be turned EVERY hour, and the lesions will be treated twice a day. Each time he is turned, we will check to be sure that the area is dry and clean. We definitely do not want an infection to set in, because that would become a whole new set of problems."

He apologized again to us because your father and I had clearly been upset; and honestly, the thought of neglect was disappointing. Careful not to sound as if he was minimizing your situation, Teddy explained that your case of bed sores was somewhat mild. However, it would in fact take some time for them to fully heal. You were still and quiet throughout the entire ordeal, just soaking it all in with a blank look on your face. I was sure you'd have your own version of this situation later, and I couldn't wait to hear it. *But, Jesus…what else can happen?*

# DAY 22

## STRONGER THAN YESTERDAY

Your night nurse Brandi called first thing in the morning and told me that you had struggled overnight. You did not sleep at all, and you asked for Dilaudid every 45 minutes! This drug is a narcotic that is in the opioid class, and it works on certain parts of the brain to change how your body feels and responds to pain. When Brandi said that you kicked and moaned most of the night, my heart dropped at the thought of how much you were suffering. It CAN'T be normal for you to be in this much discomfort! Something has to give. I demanded that the doctor be notified and requested that they revisit the regimen of pain medication that you were being given. This was ridiculous!

When we arrived at the hospital, you were chilling! As long as you'd been a patient, I thought we'd seen and worked with all of the ICU nurses by this point. Several of them had been in rotation over the last few weeks, and everyone had become pretty familiar with you, and us them. Therefore, I was surprised to see a new nurse in your room. Angie greeted me and pleasantly explained that they'd increased your Oxycodone to 20mg and stopped the Dilaudid shots altogether. There was also an additional medication that they were considering giving you in a pill form, but for the life of me, I couldn't keep track of the name of yet another drug. Nonetheless, you were relaxing hard and resting well. When I stepped up to your bedside and said, "It's good to see you," you responded with your famous comeback line..."It's good to be seen!"

You became very emotional later in the day when you

started to remember that you had a job and co-workers that you actually loved. It was just a matter of time when this topic would come up, and it was hard to find the words to discuss it with you. The best thing we could do was simply allow you to talk about it and search your memory bank for all the things that you missed.

On the day you were shot, you had worked a full day. You'd apparently spoken with your father that afternoon, and you later shared that this conversation was basically your last memory from that day.

But for me, I was pleasantly surprised to see your name and baby picture illuminate the screen of my cell phone that evening. Young people today generally send text messages to communicate, and you were no different...not even with your own mother. But that evening, something was different. It had just begun to get dark, when a warm summer rain started to hit the windshield of my date's SUV, and I was engaged in light, much needed, flirty conversation. But I excused myself and quickly explained that my son was calling, and I needed to answer the phone. Without hesitation, my new love interest quickly agreed and strongly encouraged me to take the call. "Hey, Ma! Whatcha doing?!" Your voice was cheerful, excited, and genuinely loving. I told you that I was on a date with the guy whom you'd recently met by accident just a couple of weeks prior.

I wasn't quite ready for the two of you to meet and nervously tried to scurry him out of the house when I knew you were on your way home. But we were too late! As soon as we flung open the front door to abruptly end our in-house date, you were walking up the driveway. BUSTED! The impromptu meeting went awkwardly well, however. You towered over him while smiling and shaking his hand. "Cam, this is my friend, Tom. Tom this is my baby boy, Cam." You'd both heard so much about the other, so it was almost like you already knew one another. You were happy for me, rooting for a successful relationship, and simply tickled to finally meet this mystery man.

"Oh yea? Where are y'all going?" you asked with excitement. Though I explained to you that we were heading to Virginia to try a new restaurant, you seemed to be more excited to share the details of your workday with me. You described a new skill that you learned at the paint store that day and expressed just how much you liked being an apprentice to some of your more seasoned colleagues. You sounded so happy as you discussed looking forward to a possible career with the company and furthering your trade.

I was happy FOR you and felt a sense of relief that you were starting to settle down in something positive and productive. You continued by telling me how tired you were, but you'd promised your "lady friend" (as you would refer to the girls) that you'd take her to the movies that night. You were exhausted just thinking about how you'd have to go home to shower, change, drive to Laurel to pick her up, and then sit through a 2-hour show at a Bowie theater. I reminded you that it was okay to say "no" sometimes and just rest. But you were in such a good mood, it was Friday, and it was your pay day. For a 19-year-old kid, you were on top of the world.

I didn't want to end our call, but we both knew it was time to hang up so we could continue with our planned evenings. "I love you, Ma. Have fun and be safe."

"You be safe, too...and I love you more."

Sadly, as a result of the shooting, you don't remember

this conversation at all. But I will hold on to it forever. I will always remember what a good place you were in at that moment. It made me happy enough for the both of us.

Once David arrived at the hospital, you cried almost nonstop throughout the duration of his visit. You told him several times, "I MISS YOU." Your brother continuously wiped your tears and talked to you calmly…maintaining his composure and the steadiness that you so needed. He fed you ice chips, and eventually, the two of you were talking, laughing, listening to music, and reminiscing, while you crossed your legs…just like you were in the living room at home. *You're truly a miracle, Cameron.*

We requested that Angie continue to be your nurse for as long as she was working in your POD. Her attentiveness had been amazing, to say the least. She'd been turning your body every hour on the hour, administering medication, checking on you regularly, allowing you to rest…and she even cheerfully changed your pads after a couple of accidents. She decided to remove your "condom" catheter because you now felt the sensation to pee and could actually SAY when you had to urinate.

*You had a great day, son. I will pray that you rest well tonight, with little pain, and much peace. We love you. Until tomorrow…*

*#CamStrong*

# DAY 23

## MORE THAN JUST A JOB

You were the last thing that I thought about before closing my eyes each night, and the very first thing on my mind as soon as I realized that I was awake each morning...before even opening my eyes. Specifically, that morning, the emotions you had shared about your job lingered in my spirit, and as a mother, I'd been praying on how to bring you some peace. I sat up in the bed to scroll through my texts and phone log, thinking on what to do. *I'VE GOT IT!* I immediately called your father to propose the idea of stopping by your place of business on my way to the hospital, and he confirmed that it was a good plan. I knew that my detour would cause you to wonder why I wasn't bright-eyed and bushy-tailed in time for my regularly scheduled visiting hour. But the temporary delay was sure to be well worth the wait.

I had an extra spring to my step as I got dressed, yet I couldn't help but allow my excitement to be clouded with some uncertainty. I wasn't quite sure how your coworkers would receive me. In order to make a good impression on your work family, I actually put on REAL clothes today. I found a pair of nice black jeans to squeeze into, along with a button-up blouse, complementing the ensemble with a little matching lipstick to nicely bring it all together. The rediscovered efforts in my personal preparation felt good, and I actually missed getting "dolled up" to please no one other than ME.

*NOTE TO SELF: Start putting on lipstick again every day.*

I practiced what I'd say to your supervisor in the mirror until I felt more comfortable, the same way I'd rehearsed many other important conversations with friends, coworkers, family members, or lovers. I'm a perfectionist. And though I'd heard a lot about this group of people, in reality, they were strangers to me.

I heard a bell chime when I walked through the front door of the store. I guessed this was the mechanism used to alert the employees who were working in the back room that a customer had come in. As I approached the counter, I carefully passed several rows of neatly stacked paint cans, buckets, and other supplies. The store was somewhat busy. I remembered how you used to talk about many of the same contractors who would often come in to use their business accounts to secure needed materials for industrial projects. You had become familiar with them too and had built a good working rapport. Two employees were helping customers, while another person stood patiently, awaiting his turn for assistance. Because I was not a "customer" and not interested in making a purchase or asking any questions about what type of paint to use to cover my bathroom walls, I just perused the shelves of many paint brushes and accessories that I never even knew existed.

Finally, I heard someone ask, "Ma'am, can I help you?" I recognized the mild voice from the day that I called to find out if you were at work. I immediately, I knew that this was the voice of your supervisor. He gave me a questionable look when I said, "Hi, you must be Grant." I can only imagine what crossed his mind for that millisecond! I continued by extending my arm to shake his hand, "I'm Donna, Cameron's mother."

Grant's look instantly changed from *who is this woman?* to *thank goodness you're here!* "OHHHHH, my God! Hello!

How are you? How is Cam?! I'm so glad you stopped by!"

I couldn't answer his questions fast enough before he turned to yell in the direction of his colleagues, telling them who I was. The young, thin, Black gentleman who was wearing the required blue logoed polo shirt came bouncing from behind the cash register, politely excusing himself from the customer whom he had been helping at the time. Before a word left his mouth, he hugged me like he could've been my own son. "Hi, Ma'am, I'm Benjamin. Cam has been like a little brother to me! I've been thinking about him, wondering how he was doing, but I didn't have your phone number. I'm so glad you're here! How is my man doing?!" Brad had the biggest smile on his face, and his voice was overwhelmingly sincere. I gave him and Grant a detailed update about all that you'd endured, right in the middle of the store floor, as they hung on to my every word and customers waited patiently.

Grant retreated to the back momentarily and reappeared with one of the company's regional managers. Sam was traveling the east coast locations that week and just happened to be visiting YOUR location today. What were the odds? Sam was a tall, Black, middle-aged male, who wore a pair of crisp slacks and a light-colored dress shirt, and made a beeline to where I was standing. He extended his arm to shake my hand and thanked me profusely for coming in. He'd heard a lot about you prior to your injury, and you had been described as a bright kid who was a hard worker. He talked about the one time he'd met you and said that you seemed to take a great deal of interest in learning new things and enjoyed being a part of the team. He was impressed with your manners, professionalism, and overall personality. Sam was genuinely sorry to hear what had happened to you and guaranteed that your job with the company would be waiting for you once you were ready to return to work. I certainly appreciated his kind words and knew that this would be music to your ears.

Sam and I walked down the sidewalk of the local strip mall and stepped inside the doors of a popular pizza carry-out that was nearby. He'd offered to provide lunch for our family for the day, and said it was his pleasure and the very least he could do. While I waited in the common area for my order to be called, Benjamin walked in with two large envelopes and handed them to me with a huge smile on his face. "Ms. Daniels, here are a couple cards for Cam. They're from all of us at the store. Please tell him that we love and miss him and let him know that I've been praying for him. Tell him that we're going to hang out when he gets better." I thanked Benjamin and gave him a hug and assured him that I would give you the message, as well as the cards.

"NUMBER 46!," the cashier yelled from the counter. I handed over my pre-paid ticket, grabbed two large pizzas, a large Caesar salad, and a 2-liter Sprite, and then I walked to my car. Before I could pull off, I just sat for a few minutes to gather my thoughts and allow my spirit to absorb all the love and support that was passed on from your work family. It was a lot to take in. And I knew that it would be a lot to transfer on to you. Would you realistically be able to return to your job? And if so, when? In what capacity? No one really knew what to expect in your recovery process, and we certainly couldn't predict what a work-life would look like for you in the future. But, without further ado…I shifted the gear to DRIVE and let my car take me to the hospital.

When I arrived at the hospital, my first stop was the ICU waiting room to arrange the donated lunch onto our reserved table in the back corner. Nana and Granddaddy came in right behind me with a homemade meal but decided to partake in the pizza instead. We could eat their intended lunch later on for dinner, and it would work out perfectly! Meanwhile, your father was in your room, and you both were awaiting my arrival. I scarfed down a slice of pizza before wiping my mouth and mentally preparing myself to be the bearer of happy and sad news...depending on who was asking. Somehow, I suspected it would be a mix of each emotion for you.

When I walked into the room, your eyes shifted in my direction, and you gave me a little smile. I could almost SEE your mind wondering, "Why are you late today?" I kissed you on your forehead, "Hi, Cam! I have a surprise for you!" Your eyes remained as focused on me as they could and looked like slits. I could tell that your curiosity was exactly where I wanted it to be, even though you couldn't show much expression. "Hi, Ma."

I explained that the reason I was late was because I'd stopped by your job on my way to the hospital, and I had spoken with your coworkers. Your eyes opened a little wider and no longer looked like you were still trying to wake up. "REALLY?!"

"Yep. I saw Grant, Benjamin, and Sam."

Your face lit up, then began to break up. "Benjamin?! You saw Benjamin?!" You began to cry and could barely utter another word from your mouth. Your father and I looked at one another, and with telepathy, we both wondered if I should continue talking about my visit. I motioned to him with my eyes, asking him if he thought I should read the cards that your co-workers sent. And with no hesitation, your father nodded in approval.

I proceeded to read both of the cards and each of the handwritten sentiments noted by your colleagues. With every name I called, you became more moved. You eventually began to cry uncontrollably and yell out Benjamin's name a number of times. Just as he had told me, you and Benjamin were definitely very close, and he was clearly your favorite. You loved that job, and I vowed to keep you connected to those people throughout your recovery process. They were important to you, and part of my new prayer would include your return to your workplace someday. But for now, we'd positioned the portable fan to blow directly onto your head while I wiped your face with a cool compress to calm you down. I again fought back my own tears so that I could instead offer you encouraging words. "You'll get back to your life, Cam. I promise."

# DAY 24

## THE ONLY WAY OUT IS THROUGH

Erica called this morning like clockwork. She said that you had slept pretty well during the night but woke up a couple times to ask for pain medication. Overall, you were doing okay.

The doctors would continue to experiment with the dosages of your pain medication, until they landed on the perfect combination. The goal was that you would be taking everything through the feeding tube in your stomach. You were still getting injections of the Dilaudid, but much less of it…thank goodness.

In addition to your neck, you'd also started to complain quite a bit about pain in your collar bone. Dr. Arrington was today's attending physician and had taken a personal interest in figuring out what was causing this new discomfort. He ordered an MRI to specifically look at the areas in question for potential fractures caused by the car collision. But when the results showed no existing damage, he leaned toward stiffness as the diagnosis, caused from being in bed for so long. The usual muscles that you'd use under normal circumstances were sitting dormant and, therefore, had become hardened, rigid, and inflexible.

Your father pulled a heating pad from his bag that he had brought from home and asked Angie if she could heat it up in the microwave. Repeatedly laying this warm compress across your neck kept you still and allowed you to sleep for most of the day. You gave Angie a dirty look each time she interrupted your rest to turn your body every hour, administer your scheduled medications, and simply check on you. Your brother stopped by for a little while before getting on the road for school, and your grandparents came by as well for their almost daily check-in, but Angie warned everyone not to stir you up too much. The woman was very attentive, and I appreciated her bedside manner more than she knew.

For the first time in weeks, you noticed the television that hung in the upper right corner of your room. For some time, you'd been unable to open your eyes, let alone shift them around to see everything in your peripheral. But today, you surprisingly asked if you could watch TV, and I honestly wondered just how long you'd known it was there. Maybe you just didn't feel up to it, or your eyes simply could not focus enough to see any images displayed on a television, especially from that distance. Nonetheless, I scrambled for the remote control in excitement, overjoyed that you had made the request. This was progress! Without even asking, I had my mind set on finding one of your favorite channels: ESPN or NFL Network. At home, you would leave the TV on one of these stations all day and all night, listening to related reports and updates even in your sleep. In normal circumstances, you could rattle off statistics from any and every sport and fact check news on almost every athlete, both professional and up and coming. Your mind was like the walking encyclopedia edition of a *Sports Illustrated* magazine collection, and you aspired to someday secure a career as a communicator in this industry.

"Aww, man." I repeatedly pressed the power button to no avail. Your father stood on a chair to directly press the buttons on the television but found no success with that method either. The disgusted pout on your face reminded me of the one you used to give me as a little boy when I took away your wrestling action figures as a form of temporary punishment. Each time, it was the worst moment of your life, and the world would soon end in unimaginable terror. I notified Angie that there was a problem with your television, and she promised you that she would submit a request to have it fixed. But she was transparent in further explaining that the engineers did not frequently service this area of the hospital. I guess it wasn't very common to have an ICU patient express interest in watching TV; therefore, the over-sized boob tube was pretty much on display for decoration, whether it properly functioned or not.

"I have to do #2," you announced with no shame later that evening. That was our cue to step out the room for a while for some air, and possibly a bite to eat. Angie brought in a bed pan, anticipating a normal bowel movement, and planned to give you some much deserved privacy. Though you had the urge, the high doses of narcotics in your body had finally taken their toll, causing you severe constipation. When your father and I returned almost 45 minutes later, you still had not completed the task at hand, and you were begging Angie for an enema once she made it an available option. You were visibly frustrated and began to loudly plead for the nurses to get this show on the road. Your father and I waited outside the room as Angie led the other nurses in the grueling process, and we began to hear your moans of massive pain almost immediately. You were so loud that other patients wondered what was happening, and the ICU staff in the common area had a look of concern on their faces. It was too much for me to bear, so I decided to return to the waiting room. It sounded as if someone were killing you, and I just couldn't take hearing you in so much agony. Thirty minutes and three big bowel movements later, you were exhausted, and just wanted to rest through the remainder night. What an ordeal! *You are truly #CamStrong.*

# DAY 25

## PRICELESS!

Like clockwork, my cell phone buzzed on my nightstand. And like most mornings, I wasn't asleep. Instead of lying still with my eyes closed, I tried to fathom just how much my life had changed. It was almost unreal how entirely different things could be at the blink of an eye, without any fair warning. Then all of a sudden, you were preparing for a totally unfamiliar way of living.

A popular entertainment group had recently started a new trend at the start of the summer to give hundreds of people in the community a weekly outlet that was fun, relaxing, and free of charge. Various bands were scheduled to perform, and locals gathered in the parking lot of a neighborhood strip mall, popped up their lawn chairs, brought personal coolers full of food and spirits, and simply enjoyed being outside. I'd attended this "Wind Down Thursday" event only once so far, but I had recently re-stocked my bar, looking forward to next week's outing with friends.

I'd reserved a table for 10 and a hotel room to attend the annual Pink & White Party that pays homage to breast cancer survivors and celebrates the memories of those who lost their battles. This event was important to me because it allows me to honor my deceased sister-in-love who'd succumbed to her illness several years ago. My girlfriends and I always had a good time at this function, and this year's entertainment featured Stokely from the popular R&B group, Mint Condition. I'd never seen them in concert before, so I was definitely looking forward to this summer tradition.

I'd reserved a beach house rental near the Atlantic City boardwalk. A good friend had offered me a great deal for a quick weekend *Baecation*, and I was looking forward to treating Tom to good time as we closed out the summer. Taking short trips together was on our immediate "To Do" list as we continued to reacquaint ourselves and get to know one another better.

Two months ago, I had bought tickets to the Jay-Z/Beyoncé concert in Miami, and this was the date of my early morning flight. I wasn't really a huge fan of either phenomenon but enjoyed listening to their music sometimes. They'd started their "On the Run" Tour, and it was a rare chance for a well-deserved girls' trip, so...what the hell? My hotel suite on the beach had been secured for me and my best friend, Kisha. And I'd felt like a college girl, tickled with the idea that a candy apple red Mustang convertible was reserved in my name at the car rental counter in the airport. I had a full mental list of shoes, both comfortable and club-style, that I'd pack for the trip; and I knew exactly what "come and get me" dresses would hug the perfect curves that I'd worked so hard to develop over the last year.

I'd made three installments to my girlfriend who was a travel agent for another once in a lifetime opportunity...a trip to Thailand for the coming February. The journey included time spent in Bangkok and Phuket over a 10-day period with a frequent travelers' club that I so desperately wanted to become a part of. Though I didn't know exactly what to expect, I had done much of my own research and was mentally preparing myself for the adventure, as well as for the next part of my life.

All. Cancelled.

As I lay in bed awaiting your morning report, I stopped

to carefully outline what God must have in store for my life. I'd finally finished grieving a failed marriage that I should've ended years ago and spent the necessary energy to sow my oats…so it was now time to spread my wings. But instead of becoming the audacious, carefree divorcee that I seemingly had my heart set on, other plans had already been ordered for the next steps of my journey. But a caregiver? Me? Why, Lord? What has my son done to deserve this? What have *I* done to deserve this? Things had just started to re-shape for me. My career was at a great place. My credit had been restored. And I'd just found a good man.

Just as I'd begun part my lips to ask "WHY" out loud, a single tear rolled down the side of my face. It was at that moment that I realized none of the things that I was forced to sacrifice remotely compared to the miracle that I'd been witnessing right before my eyes over the last few weeks. I had seen things that would make a non-believer BELIEVE. I'd learned more about the human brain and how it affects the body than the average person would ever willingly know. I had been exposed to a whole new world that I was unaware even existed, and the lens through which I looked at life was totally different. My purpose had shifted whether I wanted it to or not, but the value attached to the acquired nuggets along the way were PRICELESS.

## DAY 26

# THE SEARCH FOR A NEW HOME

"Hello?"

"Good morning, Donna, this is Erica, calling from Prince Georges Hospital Trauma Unit. Cameron had a good night..."

When Erica called this morning to give me your stable report, I asked her to remind you that your father and I would get to the hospital a little later than normal today because of our scheduled visits at rehabilitation hospitals. I also asked her to leave a message for Angie, requesting that she call me with a late-morning update.

Shortly after your status had been upgraded from critical condition to serious, the case manager gave me a heads up on what to expect after leaving the Intensive Care Unit of the hospital. She'd advised me to begin looking into local rehabilitation hospitals, which I later learned would be your next second home, literally. You'd live at this facility full-time for an extended period, where you'd learn how to function again, including walk, talk, eat, and all the normal things that we so often take for granted.

The Trauma Center had saved your life and nursed you back to health as much as they could. But their staff couldn't do much more for you. The expectation was that you would be moved to "the floor," as it was called, meaning the regular part of the hospital. But I clearly expressed to Ms. Monroe that I absolutely did not offer my approval in having you moved, and I wanted you to stay in ICU, leaving ONLY to be transported directly to a rehabilitation hospital. Because of Theresa's compassion, moving you was never spoken of again. However, I exercised much due diligence in researching local facilities and scheduling site visits with three locations. We had appointments at two properties today, and one tomorrow. I wanted to have a solid plan in place once the orders were approved to release you from the hospital, and I had a feeling that that day was coming sooner than we thought.

Our first stop was the National Rehabilitation Hospital (NRH), located directly across the street from Washington Hospital Center. It's a MedStar medical facility, and services many of the veterans who are discharged from the nearby Veteran Affairs Medical Clinic. We had no idea what to expect, but upon walking through the front door, we were impressed with the high glass ceilings that allowed the building to be filled with natural light. We also paid close attention to the heavily manned security desk that was guarded by two officers, who required us to show identification and sign a book to document that we were there. Considering you were a victim of a violent crime and your assailant(s) still had not been apprehended, we liked the idea of having you in a secure building with needed precautions in place.

We met with a young woman from the Admissions Office who asked me to complete some standard paperwork before giving us a full tour of the establishment. The facility had three floors of patients, who were sectioned off according to injury and needed rehabilitation. There was a specific Stroke & Brain Injury Unit that you would live in, receiving speech, occupational, and physical therapy five times per week. The hallways were clean, and the rooms were spacious enough for a provided wheelchair, television, closet space, nightstand, hospital bed, and a sitting area for visitors. Private bathrooms were in each room, equipped with a sitting shower, toilet area, and a full sink…again, large enough for a wheelchair and a few people who may need to assist the patient.

Our tour guide led us outside to the back of the building, where a large, well-maintained garden was beautifully laid out in the middle of fountains, several wrought iron benches, and tables. This was a quiet, peaceful area where residents could enjoy visits with loved ones, just to get some fresh air outside of the usual four walls. We were introduced to the therapy pool, as well as to a variety of equipment that filled the large, bright exercise rooms. There was even a separate outpatient gym that prior residents could come back to use after their discharge.

After seeing all of this, I think the area that blew us away most was the part of building that was solely designated for patients who were preparing for discharge. I couldn't get over the mock-kitchen that allowed patients to practice moving around the stove and cabinets, or the staged bedroom that gave patients a chance to get in and out of bed on their own. The simulated restaurant included menus and booths that gave patients the feel of being in a public place again; and lastly, the empty car allowed patients to routinely work on getting in and out of the passenger seat without falling, hitting their heads, or worse.

We were sold! But were looking forward to seeing what the other facilities had to offer to our son.

Next, we arrived at the historic Washington Adventist Hospital for our scheduled appointment. Entering this building was a very different experience from the one at the facility we'd just left. The ceilings were high, and our voices echoed off the walls that were filled with religious paintings and symbols. We stopped at the small information desk to ask for instructions on how to find where we needed to be, and the poor lady who seemed almost as clueless as we were muddled her way through some unsure directions. We eventually found the elevators that she mentioned at the end of the long hallway and hit the button for Level 4 upon hesitantly entering.

On the short ride up the elevator shaft, your father and I looked at one another in agreement…already, this was nothing like the other hospital. However, we both wanted to keep our minds open and give each option a fair assessment. I pulled my notebook from my purse again and flipped to the list of pre-prepared questions, all of which were fully answered to our satisfaction by the tour guide at NRH. Once the rattling elevator doors opened, we gingerly stepped off into a quiet, dim hallway. As someone who has worked in the logistics and event planning industry for a number of years, I always look for directional signage. It's one of the standard "things to do" on my checklist for any assignment no matter the size or deemed importance. People appreciate this seemingly small gesture because, in the long run, it eliminates much confusion and room for error. My eyes squinted to carefully scan the closed-in walls, and it quickly became apparent that there was no one on the architectural staff who thought like me. "Are we in the right place?"

We began our self-guided search for someone to talk to and stumbled upon a huge war room-style Nurses' Pool, filled with stacks of folders, papers, books, and people who seemed unengaged and uninterested that we'd been standing in front of them for several minutes. I was pretty sure it was obvious that we were visitors of some sort and needed assistance. Though no one was within earshot, I didn't think it would be appropriate to use my Capitol Heights voice in a hospital to demand some attention. The look on my face probably said otherwise. Finally, a nurse who was passing by stopped as she walked in our direction, "Are you guys being helped?"

*Did it LOOK like we were being helped?* "No, ma'am. We have a 12:00 p.m. appointment for a site visit." I gave her the name of the person I'd spoken to over the phone to schedule the meeting, and we were told that they were not on the schedule to work today. *UGH.* The random nurse disappeared into the pool of papers and chaotic chatter, and a small young Latina woman later emerged to reluctantly take us on a tour and answer our questions.

As we began to follow her down the hallway, we exchanged pleasantries and introductions. Two seconds later, I wouldn't have been able to remember her name if someone told me that my life depended on it. The first, second, and third impressions had lost me, and I was simply going through the motions at this point. Nurse X showed us a resident room where you'd be staying, and we immediately noticed that it was for single occupancy. This was a plus, considering NRH housed patients with roommates, unless a family had long money and was willing to pay an astronomical fee for their loved one to reside in a single suite.

Our temporary pleasure quickly turned into another downer when I inquired about the bathroom, and Nurse X described the shared bathroom that was located at the end of the hallway. *Huh? No, thank you,* I thought to myself, feeling like this was more like a glorified college dormitory. And from the look on your father's face, his thinking wasn't much different.

We continued further down the hallway until we reached the Therapy Room that was maybe a little larger than my living room at home. Out-dated exercise equipment lined the colorful walls, but our impromptu tour guide presented it like Vanna White would have done a top-of-the-line home gym on Wheel of Fortune. *Again…uhm, no.*

"This concludes our tour today. Do you have any questions for me?" Nurse X asked, clearly looking as if she hoped we would not ask any questions.

"Where is the pool that patients use for aquatic therapy," I inquired, still trying to give the facility a ray of hope.

The small-framed woman probably didn't intend to chuckle out loud, but her amusement managed to slip out. "Oh, we don't have a pool. Everything I've shown you on this floor is the rehabilitation portion of the hospital."

As we were directed back toward the elevators, we stopped at the Nurses' Pool and waited while our tour guide dug through mounds of folders to find a brochure for us. We thanked her for her time and were on our way out in less than 20 minutes flat…10 of which comprised of us standing around awaiting assistance. We were totally unimpressed, and it was a definite "no" for us. You were already entering a depressed mental state, so you needed to be in an upbeat, less depressing environment. It looked and felt lonely here, and I thought we were making the best decision to rule out this option on your behalf.

On our way to the hospital, your father and I compared mental notes and ideas. For once in a very long time, we were on the same page, agreeing that there was no need to look any further. We both loved NRH and felt that it would be the best place for you to successfully thrive. I scrolled through the pictures that I'd taken with my cell phone and was excited to share the visual and verbal overview with you. The only piece that concerned me was the investigative process that the administration was required to conduct prior to accepting your application. Because you were the victim of a violent crime, and the related case remained open with no arrests, your residence there was a potential safety risk. But as your mother, I pleaded with the necessary staff at the conclusion of our visit, asking that the decision-makers show compassion for my son. The rest was in God's hands, and so we waited.

"Hi, Cam!" You smiled at us when we entered the room, anxious to hear about what would be next for you.

# DAY 27

## IT'S THE LITTLE THINGS

Erica gave the same nightly report as she did the day before. You were doing really well. You had two small bowel movements, each becoming much easier than the last. Under normal circumstances, this wouldn't be news. However, your nurses knew that even the simple things weren't simple and definitely worth reporting.

Angie called me at about 9 a.m. shortly after she began her shift, and before I started out for the hospital. She must've heard the fear in my voice when I answered the phone, because it was not routine to receive a second morning call. She immediately said, "There is no emergency. Cameron just asked me to call to find out what time you are coming." I chuckled and sighed with relief in the same breath. *That kid!* Why did he need to know exactly what time I was coming? Was he going somewhere? "Please let him know that I'm leaving home now, and I should be there in an hour." When I did arrive, you were sitting up in bed, talking, and looking like yourself. You were ready for the day and anxious for company to show off how well you were doing. I was definitely impressed!

Your speech therapist paid you a visit early afternoon and was also very impressed with you. Leslie not only gave you ice chips, but also apple juice, apple sauce, and WATER! She started with spoon-feeding small sips of cold water to you until she was confident that you'd mastered it. Then soon afterwards, she held the paper cup up to your mouth and allowed you to take small swallows in 30 second intervals, making sure each gulp went down the correct tube! Leslie was visibly and verbally fascinated with your progress, celebrating you with praise, smiles, and giggles, all of which egged you on to do more. "So when can I eat some Five Guys," you jokingly asked with a straight face. We all let out booming laughter, giving you more ammunition to perform for us. Leslie finally controlled her amusement enough to explain that she wanted to see you a couple more times before making any further adjustments to your diet. You were satisfied with her answer, and which gave you something to look forward to. If I knew you like I thought I did, you would definitely hold Leslie to her word.

Later that evening, a little elderly man whom we've never seen before entered your room, shuffling his feet with short, quick steps. I noticed his blue uniformed collared shirt, and the matching pants hung below his waist because of the heavy toolbelt that was obviously worn from frequent use. He was a man of few words, and simply motioned toward the hanging corner television as a way to communicate the reason for his visit. We all remained quiet as we watched little Mr. Fix-It carefully prop up his ladder and perfectly align it with the angle of his targeted project. With his mouth wide open and a suspenseful look at the front of the TV, he then slowly shifted his attention to the back, clicking the same buttons that your father tested just days before. As he descended from the ladder, he began to hum a familiar tune, signifying that he had figured out the problem that none of us had been able to resolve. We watched him shuffle out the door without a word, and we couldn't help but chuckle after he disappeared for several minutes.

The balding, gray-haired man shortly became your hero and Knight in Shining Armor when he returned to the threshold of your room bearing a replacement television!

Your straight face turned into a smile immediately after the switch was successfully made, and the power button on the remote magically worked all of a sudden. In your eyes, THIS was in some way better than a Five Guys Little Bacon Cheeseburger, loaded with all of your favorite fixings! Before I could find the arrows to scroll the channels, you immediately asked me to find ESPN. *I already knew, Son.* But strangely, most of the stations were filled with static, unavailable, or just plain uninteresting, so we landed on one of two options: CNN or Cartoon Network. What a selection! But it would have to do for the time being.

It was late, and I felt comfortable enough to leave you for the night. You'd had your scheduled dosages of pain medications for the evening and seemed to be resting well. I whispered a prayer from the foot of your bed and gently touched your bare toes with anointed oil. The sound of the TV was set on the lowest volume to be sure not to disturb other resting patients. But the rays of light projected by "Dexter's Laboratory" shone over your entire body, resembling the image of you lying in your own bed at home when I peeked in your room at night. "Sleep tight, my soldier. I'll see you tomorrow."

# DAY 28

## HOPE IS THE ONLY THING STRONGER THAN FEAR

Erica called this morning to give much of the same overnight report, which was again, music to my ears. She also told me that this would be her last assigned shift to your pod for a couple of weeks. She was certain that you'd be leaving the hospital very soon and doubted that she would see us again. *Oh no!* Erica had a deep accent that sounded as if she may be of Caribbean descent. When we first met her, I must admit that I sometimes had a difficult time making out what she was saying. However, the genuine care that she exuded for you was universal, and it was obvious that she was also a mother. The more she spoke, the more closely I listened. And before I could even notice, it was if the language barrier never existed. I appreciated everything that Erica had done for you, although she looked at it as just doing her job. But in my experience with interacting with many nurses during this short time, she definitely stood out as one who not only took an interest in a patient's care and well-being, but also in connecting with the patient's family. Because of this, I could not thank her enough for what she'd meant to me, personally. Before hanging up, Erica made me promise to give her an update on your recovery process in a few months and assured me that she'd continue to pray for you.

Upon Erica's departure, she definitely handed the "Super Nurse" baton off to one of our other favorites to care for you throughout the day...Angie. When I walked into your room, you were sitting up listening to music, resting your eyes. Your television was set to CNN, but the sound had been muted. Angie had made you almost as comfortable as you would have been lying in your own bed at home, with the portable fan hooked onto the bed rail, blowing across the side of your face.

Your ability to hear surely had not been altered because your Wolverine-like instincts were triggered before I could say a word. I don't even think you had opened your eyes when I heard you greet me, "Hi, Ma." *Wow. Did he pick up on my scent?* They say that when one of your senses is weak, another is heightened, and I've always believed this theory. You may have been unable to completely SEE straight, but you could definitely HEAR everything, and possibly even SMELL now better than ever. I planted my usual kiss on your forehead, then settled into place for the day.

When your grandparents arrived, they were anxious to tell me that they'd just run into a member of their church family in the ICU waiting room and had just spent the last 20 minutes talking with her. They continued by giving a lengthy, detailed description of Mrs. Carter until they were sure that I remembered her from one of my Sunday visits to their church. Her husband had been rushed to the Trauma Center that morning and was apparently one of your new neighbors, just four doors down. Mr. Carter was in critical condition, with complications from failing organs and conditions that I didn't completely understand.

When I later made my way back to the waiting room for a breather, I immediately recognized Mrs. Carter. She quietly sat in a wheelchair close to the front door, while many of her daughters and family members sat in the nearby chairs chatting with one another. "Hi, Mrs. Clark. I'm Donald and Diana's daughter...Donna." Her face lit up, and her mouth managed to create a fragile smile while she looked up at me. I leaned down to hug her and was able to pay forward some of the encouraging words that so many had offered to me during my own trauma. I could see the look of defeat in her face as she described her husband's grim prognosis. But she was a woman of faith, and I admired how she articulated her preparedness to accept God's will. *Talk about STRONG? My God.* I could definitely take a page out of Mrs. Carter's book.

*Deep sigh.* I just needed to sit in my unmarked reserved corner for a while and decompress. I spent some time mindlessly scrolling Facebook, glancing up at whatever was on the television, and developing a crick in my neck from dozing off while allowing my unsupported head to frequently nod. I was startled by the sound of the random door opening at the end of the row of chairs. For some reason, I thought this was a storage room of some sort because I'd never seen anyone walk through it in all of my restless days sitting in the waiting room. But through my squinted eyes, still half sleepy from my cat nap, I saw a tall Black woman wearing a free-flowing colorful duster, slowly being escorted through this door. While the door was propped open, I showed no shame in quickly adjusting my neck and widening my eyes to see what was beyond this entrance. Before the door could securely close, I managed to get a glimpse of the bland room that consisted of nothing but a desk and maybe two chairs.

*Hmmm.* I wondered where this door led to, or what was in this room. But within moments, everyone in the waiting room heard a loud scream come from behind the door. We all looked at one another in disbelief, as we then could clearly hear the woman sobbing uncontrollably. I simply could not believe that THIS was the room that family members were lured into and told of their loved one's demise. Didn't the hospital have a more private setting that separated grieving mothers, daughters, sons, brothers, fathers, and grandparents from everyone else with more than just a random door? This just seemed insensitive, and the moment lacked even an ounce of compassion.

Feeling sorry for the unidentified woman but shamefully thankful that I was never called into this room, I immediately became overwhelmed with mixed emotions. I quickly gathered my purse and left the room, in need of finding a different hiding space. This one was now tainted.

Walking with no real direction or destination, my physical exhaustion would not allow my feet to take yet another step. I found myself in the hallway that connected one part of the hospital to another, just sitting on the floor in front of a wall-to-wall window. With my knees up to my chest, almost in the fetal position, I found temporary comfort in feeling the sunlight on my face. This was all just becoming too much, and I needed to somehow restore my mental strength.

Before I could think about myself fully, I remembered that I'd forgotten to contact the insurance company to confirm coverage for the rehabilitation process. I dreaded making this call, and the selfish part of me was simply afraid of what the representative would tell me on the other end of the phone. Ms. Monroe had forewarned me about insurance limits and the possible out-of-pocket expenses that would be incurred. I had absolutely no idea how much something like this would cost, or how long your rehabilitation process would take. But I DID know that my insurance coverage was not normal.

I could hear my voice bouncing off the walls and echoing

through the empty hallway, as I timidly but thoroughly explained your status to the friendly voice that requested detailed information from me. She could hear the quiver in my tone and offered the sincerest encouragement before politely asking me to hold while she verified our coverage. Those 45 seconds felt like 45 business days of waiting for life-altering test results from a taboo clinic. But when the nice lady returned to the line, her energetic voice felt and sounded like good news was coming. "Ma'am, you have amazing healthcare coverage. I'm happy to tell you that your son will be covered 100% for 120 days of in-patient rehabilitation services. And if he reaches this maximum, but still needs more time, he can be re-evaluated for approval of additional days and treatment." *120 DAYS? FOUR MONTHS!* "Oh. My. God," was all I could part my mouth to say. I think I was in shock all over again, but the bearer of good news articulated her excitement enough for us both. And though it was probably against company policy, this apparent believer openly gave the glory to God and told me that she was honored to be the one to relay the information. I remained in the awkward position on the floor for several minutes after ending the call, crying, praying, and trying to imagine what could possibly be next. *DEEP SIGH…again.* But this time, with relief. I stood up, ready.

*What in the world?!* As Angie's shift came to an end, she was sad to tell us that she would be off for several days and imagined that this would be her last time with you. First Erica…now Angie! The band was breaking up, which created an onset of anxiety for you because you were being left behind. You became visibly upset and expressed to us just how much you wanted to leave the hospital. You and Angie had formed a bond; you were part of each other's routine for several days. You made her laugh and definitely kept her on her toes, and she knew exactly what you wanted and needed without you saying a word.

Angie, and everyone else who had come in contact with you, knew that you were ready for the next phase of your journey. As sad as we all were, we were that much more excited for you. When I gave your favorite nurse one of the green #*CamStrong* wristbands as something to always remember you by, she somberly confided in me that she had a young son at home. She couldn't imagine him having to endure what you were going through, and she cried every evening when she went to bed. You had affected her in ways that we hadn't known. And as a mother herself, she grieved over you in her own way. We will never forget this young woman.

We'd never met Catherine before she took over for the night shift. Not only was she new in the rotation for your care, but she was new to the hospital and fairly new in her profession. *Really?* We introduced ourselves to her and tried to explain "our" process as best as we could. But she was pre-occupied with trying to carefully read through all of your files and appeared to be a little overwhelmed. Somehow, I knew that it would not be a smooth night. We all expected the best care and service for you...including YOU. And as your father and I began our routine to leave for the evening, you began to complain about pain. Catherine encouraged us to go home and rest, assuring us that she was "ON IT." She promised to administer your listed dosage of medication right away. And so, we took her advice and left you for the night.

## DAY 29

# BYE, FELICIA!

I actually called Catherine at about 5 a.m. because I simply could not rest while thinking about you. Though I was hoping to get an uneventful report, deep down I knew this would not be the case. My brain wasn't quite ready to hear what your new nurse laid out for me. Luckily, you were finally asleep at the time of my call, so Catherine could freely and frankly speak to me without interruption. She told me that you yelled out for her many times during the night, not because anything was wrong, but because you were lonely. The first few times, she answered your calls almost immediately, but when you kept telling her that you were in pain, she felt that you were "crying wolf." You were antsy and overly frustrated, and just wanted someone to talk to. Catherine eventually gave you a dose of Tylenol and helped settle you down with a sponge bath.

During her time with you, she played your music and talked to you as candidly as possible, explaining that when you went to the rehab hospital, you would not have nurses at your beckoned call like you did in ICU. You would have to adjust to new rules and a different structure without throwing temper tantrums...because no one would pay attention to you, unless they were informing you that your bad behavior had resulted in an untimely discharge. *WHOA! Yes, Catherine!!!!* Just what you needed to hear to not only get you through the night, but also to prepare you better for what to expect. I thanked Catherine for her honesty and told her that I would also have a conversation with you. *My child...*

I walked through the ICU doors that morning with a

little spring to my step. I was anxious to greet you with the surprise that I was hiding in a small, red insulated cooler. In route to the hospital, I stopped at Wendy's to snag three vanilla Frosties: one for you, one for me, and one for your father. We would enjoy this tasty treat together and celebrate your ability to roll the ice cream around your mouth before successfully swallowing. The little things mattered the most! But before I could reach your room, a random nurse recognized me as your mother and said that you'd been yelling out for me. "What? What's going on?" I asked out loud to no one as I sped up my step, almost running.

I entered your room to your screaming, tear-saturated face, "MY NURSE IS HORRIBLE!" Without thinking, I threw the red cooler to the floor, along with my purse and ran to your side to calm you and make more sense of what was happening. Once again, there were no nurses sitting outside your room, so you were my only source of information at the moment. You complained about how inattentive your nurse had been and were waiting for me to arrive to make the noise that you knew I would.

It was 11 a.m., and your teeth hadn't been brushed. The feeding tube lay on your stomach, unattached to anything. And a full, solid meal was sitting on your table...obviously untouched. What were you supposed to do with THAT? I looked on your Daily Goals Board and saw that someone named Felecia was your scheduled nurse for the day. *I NEED ANSWERS!*

After finding your poor unsuspecting nurse, she quickly requested the assistance of a colleague to help bring order to the chaotic scene. First and foremost, you were totally frustrated and ready to leave this place. I was, too! Now that you had the energy and wherewithal to express yourself, every little thing set you off. Luckily, I had the turned-over, half-melted Frosty in hand. There had been some confusion around the liquid diet that you were actually approved to have, and the cafeteria had brought you a meal that was fit for your father. No one had caught or corrected the mistake, nor had anyone heard from your speech therapist yet. Therefore, the timely ice cream helped to calm you down.

Leslie finally made her rounds at about 1 p.m., and you'd never been happier to see your speech therapist - aka - trusted new friend. She profusely apologized for the cafeteria mix up and had hoped that the intended tray of liquid foods would have been a nice surprise for you. But no worries...she was here now, and she was equipped with soup, pudding, Jell-O, yogurt, and MORE ice cream! You ate almost every bite, and without hesitation, asked when you'd be able to eat again. Leslie couldn't help but laugh in celebration of your continued progress before explaining that she wanted to limit you to just one meal for the day. But she would look to possibly increase your intake for the coming days. As always, you were satisfied with her answer and thankful for her welcoming visits.

You were settling in for a nap after your meal, so your father and I stepped out to grab some lunch for ourselves. After an hour, we returned to Felecia and another nurse cleaning you up from an extremely loose bowel movement that created an unbearable stench throughout the entire common area. My Frosty and Leslie's surprise ice cream had apparently run right through you. We were asked to give the nurses some time to finish their task, change your gown, and replace your bedding. We happily obliged while pinching our noses with two fingers! But just before we stepped away, I noticed your not-so-discreet gesture, motioning for me to come closer to you. You were anxious to tell me something, and as soon as you began to whisper, the nurses re-entered the room with more soapy water and towels. We gave each other a look that we both understood and non-verbally agreed to re-visit our conversation once the coast was clear.

Thirty minutes later, you were bursting at the seams to spill your tea and get to the bottom of the rumors that Felecia had inappropriately told you about the rehabilitation hospital. She said that you would not be admitted to NRH until the person who shot you was in police custody. This information had you totally confused, angry, disappointed, sad, and clearly upset. But once again, you knew that by voicing your concern to me, the problem would soon be resolved. First of all, I assured you that your nurse was completely out of line and had no idea what she was talking about. We knew that the instigator had twisted the truth and had given you bad information. But most importantly, until that moment, you didn't even know that you'd been shot. What a complete mess! I found myself on autopilot, navigating my way back to the charge nurse's office to not only complain, but to have Felecia reassigned. I demanded that she never come near you again…or else. Within minutes, Kelly walked into your room and introduced herself to all of us as your new nurse.

*Bye, Felecia.*

Things later settled down, but you were expectedly quiet. We didn't ask you what was on your mind, and you didn't tell. We all knew what the elephant in the room was, but your father and I agreed to give you some mental space to think and allow this new information to marinate.

Your occupational therapist Jessica paid you a visit while things were pretty still, and LITERALLY worked the shit out of you. She focused mainly on your left hand and arm. Though you grunted and moaned, you were determined to lift your hand several times on her command. We were all impressed with your effort, and I personally admired how you used your anger to strengthen your physically ability. Afterwards, you were exhausted and immediately began to complain about your stomach. You suffered from diarrhea for several hours from that time on, and all I could think was that the ice cream probably wasn't the best idea. Oops! Because the unit was understaffed, your father and I agreed to help Kelly lift you several times to position you on the bed pan, clean you, and dispose of your waste. This was definitely a three-man job (maybe four) considering your size and lack of mobility. And we were all completely wiped out by the time your stomach finally settled.

After I left the hospital, your father stayed with you late into the night. Now that the cat was out of the bag, the two of you could begin having a serious conversation about what happened on the night you were rushed to the hospital as "Cincinnati Doe." How were you feeling right now? What were you thinking? Maybe you'd begin to connect bits and pieces of your memory and remember exactly what happened. The police still didn't have any concrete answers, but strongly recommended that we didn't say too much to anyone just yet. So, we were now all hoping that you could possibly shed some light on the investigation, helping to bring your assailant to justice.

# DAY 30

## THE DAY HAS FINALLY COME!

When I made the early morning call to Catherine, she told me that you had had another restless night. I was not surprised. She went into a whole story of how she thought you were being manipulative by moaning all night and asking for things. Although I knew there was so much more to your reasoning and overall story, I politely thanked her for the report. She obviously had no knowledge of your new-found information, and most likely didn't care. Further, I was too exhausted to even explain it to her. I could only imagine how you must have been feeling but was glad to know that you shared some thoughts with your father during the night.

As soon as I walked through the doors of the ICU pod at around 10 o'clock in the morning, your nurse Kelly immediately told me that you had been cleared for admittance at NRH, and they were just waiting on a bed to become available.

*YESSSS!!!!!!!*

Before I could even reach your room to tell you the good news, your father called me with an NRH Administrator on the line, who confirmed that you would be transported TODAY! I literally ran the remaining distance to your room where you were resting, and shouted "Cam, you're leaving today!" You looked at me and your face just began to break up with emotion. You cried tears of joy as I leaned over your body to give you a much-needed hug. Neither of us fully knew what to expect, but we were each grateful for this new day of uncertain opportunity. *It's going to be a good day!*

I left the hospital to go home to pack some things that you needed for the rehabilitation hospital. While en route, I called your grandparents and texted close friends to tell them the exciting news.

*NOTE TO SELF: Find toiletries, underclothes, socks, tennis shoes, and work-out clothes.*

My mind raced a million miles per minute. I stuffed as many of the needed items as I could find into a red duffle bag, but I quickly realized that most of your wardrobe consisted of fashionable apparel for photo-ops and date nights. I would just have to make a stop at the store to pick up a few gym shirts, clean underwear, and thank-you cards that I wanted to give to some of the ICU staff. I called your father and asked him to also pick up a cake, plates, and forks so that we could have a small celebration with all who played a role in traveling this part of the journey with us.

While we anxiously waited hours for the transportation team to come for you, I packed up all the greeting cards that I'd placed around your room, re-reading each of them for a second time. I carefully positioned your pictures and knick-knacks in a box, along with the inspirational poems, teddy bears, and figurines that friends had sent to the hospital for you. All of your belongings were ready for the move, and I'd already envisioned how I'd arrange it all in your new digs.

The transportation team finally arrived to the hospital at 4 p.m. A man and a woman walked in the room, both with seemingly strong physiques and dressed in dark uniforms and combat boots, rolling a tall, sturdy stretcher. They both greeted us, verifying your name and birthdate, and the woman began to explain what to expect with the transport. Still in your hospital gown, the pair coordinated to lift and move you from the bed to the gurney, securely strapping you in. The man reminded you of the required helmet, and you gave us all a disappointed look as I carefully slid it down over your head. Quickly saying our last "goodbyes" to everyone, your father volunteered to ride with you in the transport van. I rushed to retrieve my car from the parking garage to follow. We were all nervous and little anxious...but ready to go, and I couldn't believe the day had finally come. You'd literally spent 30 days in ICU, fighting for your life, your dignity, and your voice. And you left with all three.

*What an incredible miracle you are!*

If one had told me thirty days ago that a person could survive a gunshot wound to the head, I would've never believed it. You not only survived it, but you also made *me* stronger in the process. I somehow managed to maintain my sanity while watching you accomplish the impossible. And for that, while praising God for His glory and commending you on your perseverance, I can't forget the importance of also giving myself the minuscule credit that I deserve.

*NOTE TO SELF: Good job, Mom.*

# EPILOGUE

Approximately 20,000 people in the United States die each year from a gunshot wound to the head. For victims who survive the initial injury, half of them perish in the emergency room. Statistically, the overall survival rate is only about 5%; and of that small percentage, less than 3% of the survivors have a good quality of life afterward. Gunshot wounds to the head have become a leading cause of TBI (Traumatic Brain Injury), leaving some wheelchair-bound, unable to speak, or challenged with the simple daily norms that we so often take for granted.

*But God!*

The drive from Prince George's Hospital Center to National Rehabilitation Hospital (NRH) took over an hour, considering the thick rush-hour traffic in D.C. My eyes were carefully focused on the transportation vehicle that was in front of me. As far as I was concerned, it was toting the most precious cargo in the world...my baby boy. As we navigated several bumpy backroads of the city, the driver of the small white van did his best to avoid the early evening gridlock. If *I* was sweating, I could only imagine how nervous *you* were. Since your father was riding with you, I texted him a few times during the transit.

"How is he doing?"
"Is he scared?"
"Is he talking?"
"What is he saying?"

Though I'm sure Gary was sick of my constant questions, he understood and replied to each one of them. He even took pictures of you lying still in the gurney and sent them to me via text. The look of fear and uncertainty was written all over your face. But what you didn't realize was that your parents shared your feelings. We were still with you, in every sense of the term.

Finally. Your "chariot" turned into the back entrance of the building, and I continued on the main road to locate the adjacent parking garage. I barely slowed down enough to push the button on the machine to grab a parking ticket. Afterward, I quickly spun my crossover Infiniti into the first available space that I saw, caring little that I was parked way over the yellow line. I gathered the duffle bag and accompanying personal belongings that you needed and rushed up the walkway leading into the front entrance of the hospital.

The guards at the front desk were expecting me and told me that you'd just arrived at Room 320. I was sure they were accustomed to the look of frantic mothers who were looking for their children upon their initial admittance. I signed the required book, showed my driver's license to the nice gentleman on duty, and damn near ran to the elevators with several bags in tow.

By the time I arrived at the room that would later become your new chambers, you were already lying in your assigned bed, and Nurse Nancy was doing her initial assessment of you. *Wow! That was fast!* She asked a number of standard questions as she scanned your body and carefully read your files. Your father stood nearby, watching attentively. He gave me a nod as a sign of approval; everything was okay so far.

Two doctors, who reminded me of Fred Flintstone and Barney Rubble, entered the room and introduced themselves to all of us. They were responsible for conducting an in-depth assessment, testing your cognitive and physical abilities. Upon their request, you grimaced as you struggled to raise your left arm, higher than you had since being hospitalized. Your father and I were shocked! Knowing you, you were trying to impress these new doctors, and it worked. We all celebrated.

By nightfall, I'd neatly folded your clothes and put them away in your assigned closet and chest of drawers. Your shoes and toiletries were arranged so that the technicians could easily access them when it was time to help you get dressed each day. To make the room as homey as possible, I taped the greeting cards from friends and family on your side of the wall, sure not to impose on your roommate's space. I placed the framed pictures that I had brought from Bed #5 on your nightstand; the medical staff at NRH would also know who you really were when looking at them. And for the final touches, I placed the metal cross next to your pictures, and then hung the green and white #*CamStrong* sign over your headboard. *Perfect!*

You'd become irritable and visibly tired and had begun asking your father and me to turn you on your side so that you could rest. Sleeping comfortably in ICU had been nearly impossible, and your new bed didn't appear to be much more inviting. We noticed right away that your feet hung over the end of the bed, leading me to believe that you'd had a growth spurt over the last month. When Abby introduced herself to us as your night nurse, we almost immediately asked her for a bed extender to accommodate your extra-long legs.

Thank goodness your television turned on with no problem, but ironically, the volume didn't work. *What was it with the TVs in these hospitals?,* I thought. But luckily, your technician Chantel swooped in to swap out the remote control, which fixed the problem right away.

She was young, cute, and friendly, and she seemed to relate to you very well. I was not sure if you instantly warmed up to her because she resolved your television issue, but I could tell that you and Chantel were going to become good friends throughout the next phase of your recovery.

I was hesitant, but I knew that it was time to leave you for the night. Abby administered all of your listed medications, and also gave you a dose of melatonin to help you rest. You were in decent spirits, and I felt as if you were in good hands. Your father and I joined hands with you, and I led us in prayer:

"Father God, we come to you tonight to thank you. Thank you, Lord, for Cameron's LIFE! Thank you for a safe transport from one destination to another, and for a new home for our son. Thank you for his continued progress, Father God. We ask you, Lord, to take away his pain and replace it with peace tonight. Allow him to rest, without anxiety, stress, or fear. Lord, cover him in your blood, and guide the doctors, nurses, technicians and therapists, giving them the wherewithal to successfully assist our son in this healing process. And God, please calm my and Gary's spirit so that we, too, are able to rest without worry. Remind us all to lean on you, Father God, for the comfort that we need to get through the night. And we trust in you to see us through to tomorrow, Lord God. These blessings I ask in your name, Jesus Christ, Our Lord. Amen."

Your father wished you a good night, and walked out into the hallway. I stayed behind to give you one last kiss on the forehead as your eyes became even more heavy. "Good night, son. I love you."

After two long, grueling months of intense physical,

occupational, and speech therapy, Cameron walked out of National Rehabilitation Hospital without ANY assistance. Wearing his soft blue helmet and his favorite pair of faded jeans with the rips in the knees, he was without a wheelchair, walker, or cane. He re-learned how to walk, talk, eat, and more! As at Prince George's Hospital Center, he had become everyone's ray of hope at NRH, and staff from all over the building were honored to meet him. He won the hearts of his immediate medical team, who were all sad to see him go, but all cheered for him as he left. The surgeon back in ICU was right...Cameron's youth and athleticism did play a role in his rehabilitation. But what stamped it was his will to live and the grace of God. My son is a walking miracle!

# DEUTERONOMY 31:6

Be strong and courageous.
Do not be afraid or terrified because of them, for the Lord
your God goes with you;
He will never leave you nor forsake you.

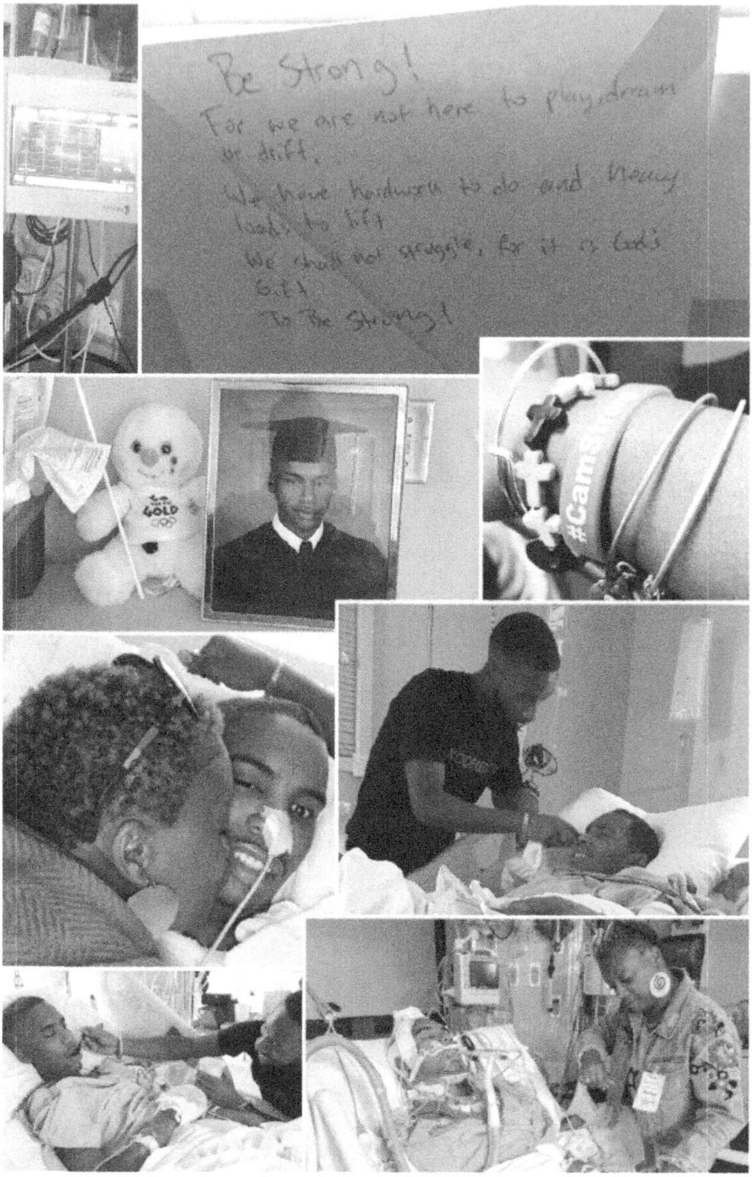
Be Strong!
For we are not here to play, dream
or drift,
We have hardwork to do and heavy
loads to lift
We shall not struggle, for it is God's
Gift
To Be Strong!
GOLD

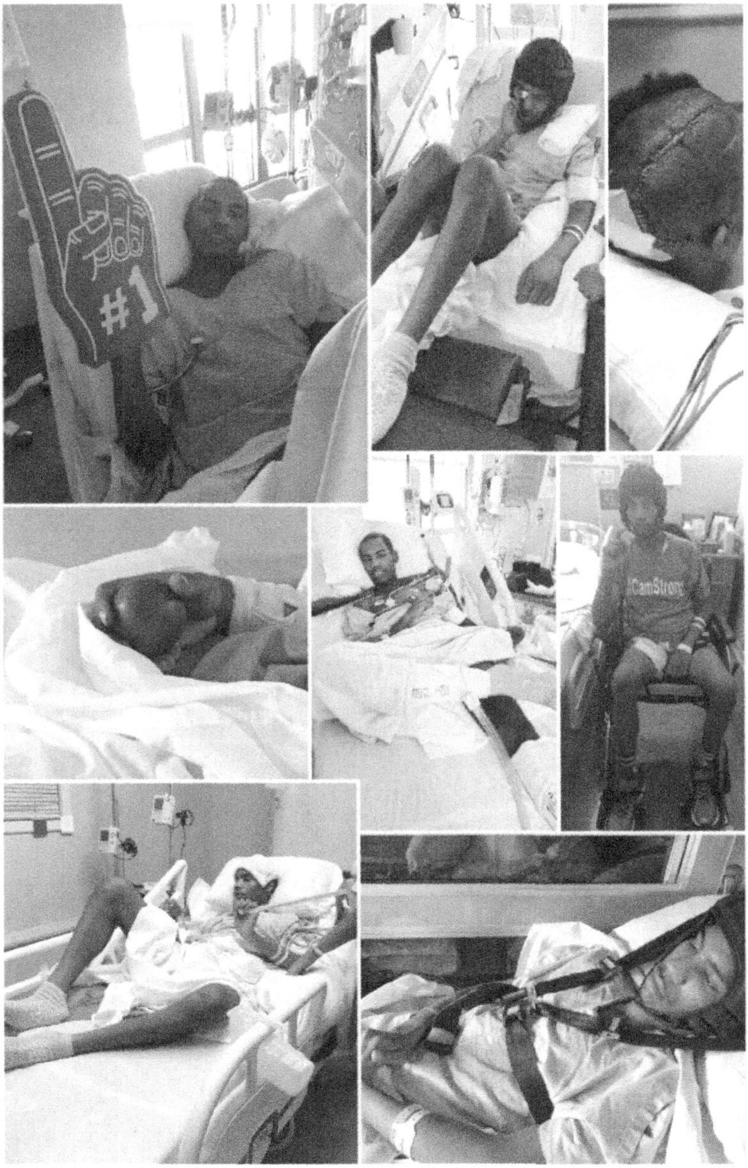
#1

#CamStrong
#CamStrong

mStrong
Welcome Home, CAM!

Made in the USA
Monee, IL
22 March 2021

62749057R00115